D1338412

A BOOK OF PEACE

Books by Elizabeth Goudge

Novels

GREEN DOLPHIN COUNTRY
THE HERB OF GRACE
GENTIAN HILL
THE HEART OF THE FAMILY
THE ROSEMARY TREE
THE WHITE WITCH
THE DEAN'S WATCH
THE SCENT OF WATER
THE CHILD FROM THE SEA

*   *   *

Omnibus editors

THE ELIOTS OF DAMEROSEHAY
THREE CITIES OF BELLS

*   *   *

Religious

A DIARY OF PRAYER
ST. FRANCIS OF ASSISI
GOD SO LOVED THE WORLD
THE REWARD OF FAITH

*   *   *

Anthology

AT THE SIGN OF THE DOLPHIN

*   *   *

Short Stories

THE LOST ANGEL

ELIZABETH GOUDGE

A Book of Peace

AN ANTHOLOGY

HODDER AND STOUGHTON
LONDON SYDNEY AUCKLAND TORONTO

Printed in Great Britain for Hodder and Stoughton Limited,
St. Paul's House, Warwick Lane, London EC4P 4AH by
Richard Clay (The Chaucer Press), Ltd., Bungay, Suffolk.

For
WINIFRED DOWN

ACKNOWLEDGMENTS

Acknowledgment is gratefully made for permission to include the following works or extracts from them:

Ana, Marcos: *A Short Letter to the World* (from FROM BURGOS JAIL, translated from the Spanish by Chloe Vulliamy and Stephen Sedley, published by Appeal for Amnesty in Spain).

Blunden, Edmund: *Almswomen* (from THE WAGGONER AND OTHER POEMS, published by Sidgwick & Jackson Ltd., by permission of the Author's Representatives and the publishers).

Bolt, David: *The Peace of Eden* (from ADAM, published by J. M. Dent & Sons Ltd.).

Bridges, Robert: *Absence* (from the OXFORD BOOK OF ENGLISH VERSE, published by the Clarendon Press).

Carmichael, Alexander: *Three Blessings* (translated from the Gaelic, from THE SUN DANCES, published by the Christian Community Press).

Causley, Charles: *At the British War Cemetery, Bayeux* (from UNION STREET, published by Rupert Hart-Davis Ltd.).

Chalmers, P. R.: *The Badger* (published by Methuen & Co. Ltd.).

Chaucer, Geoffrey: *The Good Parson* (translated by H. C. Leonard. From THE WORLD'S GREAT RELIGIOUS POETRY, published by Macmillan & Company, New York).

Chesterton, G. K.: *The House of Christmas* (from COLLECTED POEMS OF G. K. CHESTERTON, published by Burns and Oates, Ltd.); *The Holy of Holies* (from THE WILD KNIGHT AND OTHER POEMS, published by J. M. Dent and Sons Ltd., by permission of Miss Collins and the publisher).

Davies, W. H.: *Peace and Rest, Butterflies, A Chant, On a Cold Day, The Kingfisher, The Dragonfly, The Rat, The Peacemaker, Y is for Youth* (from THE COMPLETE POEMS OF W. H. DAVIES, published by Jonathan Cape Ltd., by permission of Mrs. H. M. Davies).

de la Mare, Walter: *A Recluse, The Spectacle, Once, 'Oh heart hold thee secure', '. . . All Gone . . .'* (by permission of the Literary Trustees of Walter de la Mare, and The Society of Authors as their representative).

Dickinson, Patric: *The Redwing, Bluebells* (from THE WORLD I SEE, published by Chatto & Windus Ltd.).

Dobson, Austin : *Sat est Scripsisse, A City Flower, Urceus Exit* (from COLLECTED POEMS, published by Routledge & Kegan Paul Ltd.).

Drinkwater, John : *Moonlit Apples* (from THE COLLECTED POEMS OF JOHN DRINKWATER, published by Sidgwick & Jackson Ltd., by permission of the Author's Representatives).

Dyment, Clifford : *Holidays in Childhood* (from THE AXE IN THE WOOD, published by J. M. Dent & Sons Ltd.).

Edminson, V. L.: *Temper in October* (from POEMS OF TO-DAY, published by Sidgwick & Jackson Ltd., by permission of the author).

Firth, Peter : *To My Wife* (from 'Prism', November 1964, by permission of the author).

Gogarty, Oliver St. John : *The Image-Maker* (from COLLECTED POEMS, published by Constable & Co. Ltd.).

Graves, Robert : *Bird of Paradise, The Visitation, Mid-Winter Waking, Through Nightmare, The Climate of Thought* (from COLLECTED POEMS), *A pinch of Salt* (from FAIRIES AND FUSILIERS, published by Cassell & Co. Ltd., by permission of Mr. Robert Graves).

Griffin, Pamela : *Elegy in a Museum, The Swan's Nest* (by permission of the author).

Gwilym, Dafydd ap : *The Mass of the Grove, The Stars, A Garland of Peacock Feathers* (from MEDIEVAL WELSH LYRICS, translated by Joseph P. Clancy, published by Macmillan & Co. Ltd., by permission of The Macmillan Company of Canada and the publisher).

Hardy, Thomas : *The Oxen* (from THE COLLECTED POEMS OF THOMAS HARDY, published by Macmillan & Co. Ltd., by permission of the Trustees of the Hardy Estate, The Macmillan Company of Canada and the publisher).

Heath-Stubbs, John : *A Charm against the Toothache, Prayer to St. Lucy, Care in Heaven, For the Nativity, Through the Dear Might of Him that Walked the Waves, Canticle of the Sun Dancing on Easter Morning, Homage to J. S. Bach* (from SELECTED POEMS, published by the Oxford University Press, by permission of David Higham Associates Ltd.).

Hill, Geoffrey : *God's Little Mountain* (from FOR THE UNFALLEN, published by André Deutsch Ltd.).

Hopkins, Gerard Manley : *Ash-boughs, In the Valley of the Elwy, Heaven Haven, A Nun takes the Veil, The Habit of Perfection* (from THE COMPLETE POEMS OF GERARD MANLEY HOPKINS, published by the Oxford University Press).

Housman, A. E.: *When green buds hang, Loveliest of Trees, For my Funeral, From far, from eve and morning* (from THE COLLECTED POEMS OF A. E. HOUSMAN, published by Jonathan Cape Ltd., by permission of the Society of Authors and the publisher).

Hughes, Ted: *The Horses, Song, Griefs for Dead Soldiers* (from THE HAWK IN THE RAIN, published by Faber & Faber Ltd.).

Jammes, Francis: *Prayer to Go to Paradise with the Asses* (from THE NEIGHBOURS, translated from the French by Jethro Bithell, by permission of the Universities Federation for Animal Welfare).

Jennings, Elizabeth: *Retort to the Anti-Abstractionists, The Shells, The Visitors, The Confidence* (from RECOVERIES, published by André Deutsch Ltd.).

Joyce, James: *A Flower given to my Daughter* (from POEMS, published by Jonathan Cape Ltd., by permission of The Society of Authors as the literary representatives of the Estate of the late James Joyce).

King, Martin Luther: Two articles printed in *The Pacifist Conscience*, Chicago, Ill., in April 1960, by permission of *The Christian Century*.

Kipling, Rudyard: *The Love Song of Har Dyal* (from PLAIN TALES FROM THE HILLS); *The Recall* (from ACTIONS AND REACTIONS); *Shiv and the Grasshopper, Road Song of the Bandar Log* (from THE JUNGLE BOOK); *Eddi's Service* (from REWARDS AND FAIRIES); *The Captive* (from TRAFFICS AND DISCOVERIES) published by Macmillan & Co. Ltd., by permission of Mrs. Bambridge, the Macmillan Company of Canada and the publisher; *Gunga Din* (from BARRACK ROOM BALLADS, published by Methuen & Co. Ltd., by permission of Mrs. Bambridge, the Macmillan Company of Canada and the publisher; *All the World Over* (from THE DEFINITIVE EDITION OF RUDYARD KIPLING'S VERSE, by permission of Mrs. Bambridge and the Macmillan Company of Canada).

Kirkup, James; *A Cave, To an Old Lady Asleep at a Poetry Reading, Ghosts, Fire, Water* (from THE DESCENT INTO THE CAVE); *Landscape, by Ch'eng Sui: No. V* from *Seven Pictures from China* (from THE PRODIGAL SON); *Poem to be Cast into the Sea in a Bottle, Prayer, The Blessed Received in Paradise, Pentecost* (from THE SUBMERGED VILLAGE AND OTHER POEMS); *A Charm for the Ear-Ache* (from A CORRECT COMPASSION, published by the Oxford University Press, by permission of the author).

Langland, William: *The Harrowing of Hell* (from VISIONS FROM PIERS PLOWMAN, translated by Nevill Coghill, published by J. M. Dent & Sons Ltd.); *The Vision of the Holy Church* (from VISIONS OF PIERS PLOWMAN, translated into modern English by Nevill Coghill, published by Phoenix House).

Lawrence, D. H.: *Song of a Man who has Come Through, Baby Tortoise, Tortoise Shell, A Baby Asleep after Pain, Street Lamps, Nonentity, In Trouble and Shame, The Bride, Call into Death* (from THE COMPLETE POEMS OF D. H. LAWRENCE, published by William Heinemann, Ltd., by permission of Laurence Pollinger

9

Ltd., and the Estate of the late Mrs. Frieda Lawrence).

Lee, Laurie: *Stork in Jerez, The Long War, Deliverance, The Wild Trees* (from THE SUN MY MONUMENT, published by Chatto & Windus Ltd.); *Christmas Landscape* (from THE BLOOM OF CANDLES, published by John Lehmann Ltd.).

Lewis, Cecil Day: *'Saints and Heroes you dare say'*, extract from *Saint Anthony's Shirt, Pietà* (from THE ROOM AND OTHER POEMS, published by Jonathan Cape, Ltd., by permission of the author).

Lewis, C. S.: *'Man is a Lumpe where all Beasts Kneaded be', Poem for Psychoanalysts and/or Theologians, The Ecstasy, Posturing, The Day with a White Mark, No Beauty we could Desire* (from POEMS, published by Geoffrey Bles Ltd.).

MacNeice, Louis: *To Mary—A Dedication* (from THE BURNING PERCH, published by Faber & Faber Ltd.).

Marston, John: *A Scholar and His Dog* (from THE NEIGHBOURS, by permission of the Universities Federation for Animal Welfare).

Masefield, John: *'So in the empty sky the stars appear', June Twilight, Sonnet on the Death of his Wife, 'O God, beloved God', Here in the self is all, The Seekers* (published by William Heinemann Ltd., by permission of The Society of Authors and the late Dr. John Masefield, O.M.).

Meynell, Alice: *The Visiting Sea, A Figure of the Epiphany, The Unknown God, At Night, Renouncement* (from POEMS, published by Burns Oates & Washbourne Ltd., by permission of the Executors of Alice Meynell).

Monro, Harold: *Milk for the Cat, Harbour, Real Property, The Rebellious Vine, The Guest* (from COLLECTED POEMS, published by R. Cobden-Sanderson Ltd., by permission of The Bodley Head).

Moraes, Dom: *Song, The Final Word, The Guardians, Bells for William Wordsworth* (from POEMS, published by Eyre & Spottiswoode, Ltd.).

Muir, Edwin: *Sunset, The Horses, The Difficult Land, The Question, The Killing, To Franz Kafka, Song, The Sufficient Place, The Transfiguration, 'For Once in a dream or trance I saw the gods'* (The Labyrinth) (from COLLECTED POEMS, published by Faber & Faber Ltd.).

Murray, Gilbert: Translation of *The Hippolytus* by Euripides (published by George Allen & Unwin Ltd.).

Nicholson, Norman: *The Crocus* (from ROCK FACE, published by Faber & Faber Ltd.).

Noyes, Alfred: *The Caterpillar* (from ORCHARD'S BAY, published by Sheed & Ward Ltd., by permission of Mr. Hugh Noyes).

Owen, Wilfred: *The Calls, The Parable of the Old Men and the Young, Exposure, Strange Meeting* (from THE COLLECTED POEMS

In Church (from PIETA); *The Labourer* (from SONG AT THE YEAR'S TURNING); *The Country Clergy, Farm Wife* (from POETRY FOR SUPPER, published by Rupert Hart-Davis Ltd.).

Turner, Walter James: Extract from *The Seven Days of the Sun* (from POEMS, published by Sidgwick & Jackson Ltd.).

Tynan, Katharine: *Sheep and Lambs, The God on the Hearth, The Meeting, She Asks for New Earth, The House of Life* (from POEMS, published by Allen Figgis & Co. Ltd., by permission of the Society of Authors and Miss Pamela Hinkson).

Waley, Arthur: *The Gardener*, translated from the Chinese poem by Po-Chü-I (from 170 CHINESE POEMS, published by Constable & Co. Ltd.).

Wolfe, Humbert: *The Thought, A Chorister in Avalon, The Fiddle and the Bow, Torchbearer* (from THE UNKNOWN GODDESS, published by Methuen & Co. Ltd.).

Yeats, W. B.: *The Wild Swans at Coole, He wishes for the Cloths of Heaven, The Folly of being Comforted, When you are Old, The Magi, Sailing to Byzantium, To his Heart Bidding it have no Fear* (from COLLECTED POEMS, published by Macmillan & Co. Ltd., by permission of Mr. M. B. Yeats and the publisher).

PREFACE

To be at peace. The longing for peace must have come to us with the dawn of reason, as soon as man was able to ask himself, 'What do I want?' He knew it first perhaps in the passing of a storm, when the terrifying thunder and darkness rolled away, the sun came out on a rain-washed world and the birds sang again. Then when a fight with man or beast was over and he was still alive, and could get back to husbandry or rock-painting, work that absorbed and quieted him, made no noise and shed no blood, or when he went home at night to his cave and saw in the firelight his son asleep in the mother's arms. Or, supremely, when in a still and soundless world he waited in trembling awe for the rising of the sun, not knowing with certainty if the god would come again, only hoping, until he heard the first joyous cry of a bird and saw the slow lightening on the eastern horizon. Then would come peace, flooding his soul as the glory of his God once more dawned upon him.

Never have we longed for peace as we do now, when war has become an obscene horror worse than any imaginable storm, and noise and confusion so invade cities and homes that we are in danger of having our very minds and souls battered to a uniform pulp. But in our much greater need we turn to the same sources of peace as our forefathers did; to Janus-faced nature when it is her tranquil smile she turns to us, and not her frown, to painting or gardening or whatever creative work brings us self-forgetfulness, to fire-lit homes and all the human love and friendship they stand for. And to the peace of the eternal mystery.

The poems in this book are collected here simply because I love them all, but I have tried to arrange them in these four groups of natural beauty, peaceful work, love and home, and the mystery. So many things can come under this last heading, dreams and myths and fairy tales, and the reverence and awe and way of life with which each of us confront the mystery and to which we give the odd name of religion. Only music, art, and poetry can express our experience of mystery, and then how inadequately. And how inadequate I have felt, merely trying to choose a few poems that would express the human attempt.

There are extracts in this book that to the reader may seem out of place. But love is not all joy and peace, it can cause us the most intense suffering we know, and it is the dreadfulness of war that drives us to labour for peace. And so there are some lovers' laments here, and a few war poems. They seemed necessary by way of contrast.

16

PART I

PEACEFUL SCENES

Only the Island which we sow,
(A World without the World) so far
From present wounds, it cannot show
    An ancient scar.

White Peace (the beautifull'st of things)
Seems here her everlasting rest
To fix, and spreads her downy Wings
    Over the Nest:

As when great *Jove*, usurping Reign,
From the plagu'ed World did her exile,
And ty'd her with a golden Chain
    To one blest Isle:

Which in a Sea of plenty swam
And Turtles sang on ev'ry Bough,
A safe retreat to all that came
    As ours is now.

                Sir Richard Fanshawe

From An Ode, upon occasion of His Majesty's Proclamation in the Year 1630. Commanding the Gentry to reside upon their Estates in the Countrey

TO MR. IZAAK WALTON

Farewell thou busie World, and may
  We never meet again:
Here I can eat, and sleep, and pray,
And do more good in one short day,
  Than he who his whole Age out-wears
Upon thy most conspicuous Theatres,
Where nought but Vice and Vanity do reign.

Good God! how sweet are all things here!
How beautifull the Fields appear!
How cleanly do we feed and lie!
Lord! what good hours do we keep!
　　How quietly we sleep!
What Peace! What Unanimity!
How innocent from the lewd Fashion,
Is all our bus'ness, all our Conversation!

Oh how happy here's our leisure!
Oh how innocent our pleasure!
Oh ye Vallies, oh ye Mountains,
Oh ye Groves and Chrystall Fountains,
　　How I love at liberty
By turn to come and visit ye!

O Solitude, the Soul's best Friend,
That man acquainted with himself dost make,
And all his Maker's Wonders to intend;
　　With thee I here converse at will,
　　And would be glad to do so still;
For it is thou alone that keep'st the Soul awake.

How calm and quiet a delight
　　It is alone
　　To read, and meditate, and write,
By none offended, nor offending none;
　　To walk, ride, sit, or sleep at one's own ease,
And pleasing a man's self, none other to displease!

......

Lord! would men let me alone,
What an over-happy one
　　Should I think my self to be,
　　Might I in this desert place,
Which most men by their voice disgrace,
　　Live but undisturb'd and free!
　　Here in this despis'd recess
　　　Would I maugre Winter's cold,

And the Summer's worst excess,
Try to live out to sixty full years old,
    And all the while
    Without an envious eye
Or any thriving under Fortune's smile,
  Contented live, and then contented die.
              Charles Cotton   from The Retirement

LINES COMPOSED A FEW MILES ABOVE TINTERN ABBEY

                  The sounding cataract
Haunted me like a passion; the tall rock,
The mountain, and the deep and gloomy wood,
Their colours and their forms, were then to me
An appetite; a feeling and a love,
That had no need of a remoter charm,
By thought supplied, nor any interest
Unborrowed from the eye.—That time is past.
And all its aching joys are now no more,
And all its dizzy raptures. Not for this
Faint I, nor mourn, nor murmur; other gifts
Have followed; for such loss, I would believe,
Abundant recompense. For I have learned
To look on Nature, not as in the hour
Of thoughtless youth; but hearing oftentimes
The still, sad music of humanity,
Nor harsh, nor grating, though of ample power
To chasten and subdue. And I have felt
A presence that disturbs me with the joy
Of elevated thoughts; a sense sublime,
Of something far more deeply interfused,
Whose dwelling is the light of setting suns,
And the round ocean and the living air,
And the blue sky, and in the mind of man;
A motion and a spirit, that impels
All thinking things, all objects of all thought,
And rolls through all things. Therefore am I still
A lover of the meadows and the woods,

And mountains; and of all that we behold
From this green earth; of all the mighty world
Of eye and ear,—both what they half create,
And what perceive; well pleased to recognize
In nature and the language of the sense,
The anchor of my purest thoughts, the nurse,
The guide, the guardian of my heart, and soul
Of all my moral being.

William Wordsworth

UPON WESTMINSTER BRIDGE

Earth has not anything to show more fair:
Dull would he be of soul who could pass by
   A sight so touching in its majesty:
This City now doth like a garment wear
The beauty of the morning; silent, bare,
   Ships, towers, domes, theatres, and temple lie
   Open unto the fields, and to the sky;
All bright and glittering in the smokeless air.
Never did sun more beautifully steep
   In his first splendour valley, rock, or hill;
Ne'er saw I, never felt, a calm so deep!
   The river glideth at his own sweet will:
Dear God! the very houses seem asleep;
   And all that mighty heart is lying still!

William Wordsworth

GOD'S VIRTUE

The world's bright comforter, whose beamsome light
Poor creatures cheereth, mounting from the deep,
   His course doth in prefixed compass keep;
And, as courageous giant, takes delight
To run his race and exercise his might,

24

Till him, down galloping the mountain's steep,
Clear Hesperus, smooth messenger of sleep,
Views; and the silver ornament of night
Forth brings, with stars past number in her train,
All which with sun's long borrowed splendour shine.
The seas, with full tide swelling, ebb again;
All years to their old quarters new resign;
The winds forsake their mountain-chambers wild,
And all in all things with God's virtue filled.

Barnabe Barnes

PEACE

I seek for peace—I care not where 'tis found:
On this rude scene in briers and brambles drest,
If peace dwells here, 'tis consecrated ground,
And owns the power to give my bosom rest;
To soothe the rankling of each bitter wound,
Gall'd by rude envy's adder-biting jest,
And worldly strife—ah, I am looking round
For peace's hermitage, can it be found?—
Surely that breeze that o'er the blue wave curl'd
Did whisper soft, 'Thy wanderings here are blest.'
How different from the language of the world!
Nor jeers nor taunts in this still spot are given:
Its calm's a balsam to a soul distrest;
And, where peace smiles, a wilderness is heaven.

John Clare

Who loves a garden, loves a greenhouse too.
Unconscious of a less propitious clime,
There blooms exotic beauty, warm and snug,
While the winds whistle and the snows descend.
The spiry myrtle with unwithering leaf
Shines there and flourishes. The golden boast

Of Portugal and western India there,
The ruddier orange and the paler lime,
Peep through their polished foliage at the storm,
And seem to smile at what they need not fear.
The amomum there with intermingling flowers
And cherries hangs her twigs. Geranium boasts
Her crimson honours, and the spangled beau
Ficoides, glitters bright the winter long.
All plants, of every leaf that can endure
The winter's frown, if screened from his shrewd bite,
Live there and prosper. Those Ausonia claims,
Levantine regions these; the Azores send
Their jessamine, her jessamine remote
Caffraria: foreigners from many lands,
They form one social shade, as if convened
By magic summons of the Orphean lyre.
Yet just arrangement, rarely brought to pass
But by a master's hand, disposing well
The gay diversities of leaf and flower,
Must lend its aid to illustrate all their charms,
And dress the regular yet various scene.
Plant behind plant aspiring, in the van
The dwarfish, in the rear retired, but still
Sublime above the rest, the statelier stand.
So once were ranged the sons of ancient Rome
A noble show! while Roscius trod the stage;
And so, while Garrick as renowned as he,
The sons of Albion, fearing each to lose
Some note of Nature's music from his lips,
And covetous of Shakespeare's beauty seen
In every flash of his far-beaming eye.
Nor tastes alone and well-contrived display
Suffice to give the marshalled ranks the grace
Of their complete effect. Much yet remains
Unsung, and many cares are yet behind,
And more laborious; cares on which depends
Their vigour, injured soon, not soon restored.
The soil must be renewed, which, often washed,
Loses its treasure of salubrious salts,
And disappoints the roots; the slender roots
Close interwoven, where they meet the vase

Must smooth be shorn away; the sapless branch
Must fly before the knife; the withered leaf
Must be detached, and where it strews the floor
Swept with a woman's neatness, breeding else
Contagion, and disseminating death.
Discharge but these kind offices, (and who
Would spare, that loves them, offices like these?)
Well they reward the toil. The sight is pleased,
The scent regaled, each odoriferous leaf,
Each opening blossom, freely breathes abroad
Its gratitude, and thanks him with its sweets.

William Cowper   from Book III of The Task

NATURE'S ENCHANTMENT

To one who has been long in city pent,
　'Tis very sweet to look into the fair
　And open face of heaven,—to breathe a prayer
Full in the smile of the blue firmament.
Who is more happy, when, with heart's content,
　Fatigued he sinks into some pleasant lair
　Of wavy grass, and reads a debonair
And gentle tale of love and languishment?
Returning home at evening, with an ear
　Catching the notes of Philomel,—an eye
Watching the sailing cloudlet's bright career,
　He mourns that day so soon has glided by,
E'en like the passage of an angel's tear
　That falls through the clear ether silently.

John Keats

TO AUTUMN

Season of mists and mellow fruitfulness!
  Close bosom-friend of the maturing sun;
Conspiring with him how to load and bless
  With fruit the vines that round the thatch-eaves run;
To bend with apples the moss'd cottage-trees,
  And fill all fruit with ripeness to the core;
    To swell the gourd, and plump the hazel shells
  With a sweet kernel; to set budding more,
And still more, later flowers for the bees,
Until they think warm days will never cease,
  For Summer has o'er-brimm'd their clammy cells.

Who hath not seen thee oft amid thy store?
  Sometimes whoever seeks abroad may find
Thee sitting careless on a granary floor,
  Thy hair soft-lifted by the winnowing wind:
Or on a half-reap'd furrow sound asleep,
  Drowsed with the fume of poppies, while thy hook
    Spares the next swath and all its twinèd flowers;
And sometimes like a gleaner thou dost keep
  Steady thy laden head across a brook;
  Or by a cider-press, with patient look,
    Thou watchest the last oozings hours by hours.

Where are the songs of Spring? Ay, where are they?
  Think not of them, thou hast thy music too,—
While barrèd clouds bloom the soft-dying day,
  And touch the stubble-plains with rosy hue;
Then in a wailful choir the small gnats mourn
  Among the river sallows, borne aloft
    Or sinking as the light wind lives or dies;
And full-grown lambs loud bleat from hilly bourn;
  Hedge-crickets sing; and now with treble soft
  The redbreast whistles from a garden-croft:
    And gathering swallows twitter in the skies.

John Keats

AUTUMN

Today the peace of autumn pervades the world.
In the radiant noon, silent and motionless, the wide stillness
    rests like a tired bird spreading over the deserted fields
    to all horizons its wings of golden green.
Today the thin thread of the river flows without song, leaving
    no mark on its sandy banks.
The many distant villages bask in the sun with eyes closed in
    idle and languid slumber.
In the stillness I hear in every blade of grass, in every speck
    of dust, in every part of my own body, in the visible and
    invisible worlds, in the planets, the sun, and the stars,
    the joyous dance of the atoms through endless time—the
    myriad murmuring waves of Rhythm surrounding Thy
    throne.

Rabindranath Tagore

STANZAS

Often rebuked, yet always back returning
    To those first feelings that were born with me,
And leaving busy chase of wealth and learning
    For idle dreams of things which cannot be:

Today, I will seek not the shadowy region;
    Its unsustaining vastness waxes drear;
And visions rising, legion after legion,
    Bring the unreal world too strangely near.

I'll walk, but not in old heroic traces,
    And not in paths of high morality,
And not among the half-distinguished faces,
    The clouded forms of long-past history.

I'll walk where my own nature would be leading:
    It vexes me to choose another guide:
Where the grey flocks in ferny glens are feeding;
    Where the wild wind blows on the mountain side.

What have those lonely mountains worth revealing?
   More glory and more grief than I can tell:
The earth that wakes *one* human heart to feeling
   Can centre both the world of Heaven and Hell.

Emily Brontë

THE MOOR

It was like a church to me.
I entered it on soft foot,
Breath held like a cap in the hand.
It was quiet.
What God was there made himself felt,
Not listened to, in clean colours
That brought a moistening of the eye,
In movement of the wind over grass.

There were no prayers said. But stillness
Of the heart's passions—that was praise
Enough; and the mind's cession
Of its kingdom. I walked on,
Simple and poor, while the air crumbled
And broke on me generously as bread.

R. S. Thomas

When green buds hang in the elm like dust
   And sprinkle the lime like rain,
Forth I wander, forth I must,
   And drink of life again.

Forth I must by hedgerow bowers
   To look at the leaves uncurled,
And stand in fields where cuckoo flowers
   Are lying about the world.

A. E. Housman

Loveliest of trees, the cherry now
Is hung with bloom along the bough.
And stands about the woodland ride
Wearing white for Eastertide.

Now, of my threescore years and ten,
Twenty will not come again,
And take from seventy springs a score,
It only leaves me fifty more.

And since to look at things in bloom
Fifty springs are little room,
About the woodlands I will go
To see the cherry hung with snow.

                                        A. E. Housman

SUNSET

Fold upon fold of light,
Half-heaven of tender fire,
Conflagration of peace,
Wide hearth of the evening world.
How can a cloud give peace,
Peace speaks through bodiless fire
And still the angry world?

Yet now each bush and tree
Stands still within the fire,
And the bird sits on the tree.
Three horses in a field
That yesterday ran wild
Are bridled and reined by light
As in a heavenly field.
Man, beast and tree in fire,
The bright cloud showering peace.

                                        Edwin Muir

PEACE AND REST

Under this tree, where light and shade
   Speckle the grass like a Thrush's breast,
Here, in this green and quiet place,
   I give myself to peace and rest.

The peace of my contented mind,
   That is to me a wealth untold—
When the Moon has no more silver left,
   And the Sun's at the end of his gold.

W. H. Davies

ASH-BOUGHS

Not of all my eyes wandering on the world,
Is anything a milk to the mind so, so sighs deep
Poetry tó it, as a tree whose boughs break in the sky.
Say it is ásh-boughs: whether on a December day and furled
Fast or they in clammyish lashtender combs creep
Apart wide and new-nestle at heaven most high.
They touch heaven, tabour on it; how their talons sweep
The smouldering enormous winter welkin! May
Mells blue and snow white through them, a fringe and fray
Of greenery: it is old earth's groping towards the steep
   Heaven whom she childs us by.

Gerard Manley Hopkins

IN THE VALLEY OF THE ELWY

I remember a house where all were good
   To me, God knows, deserving no such thing:
   Comforting smell breathed at very entering,
Fetched fresh, as I suppose, off some sweet wood.
That cordial air made those kind people a hood

All over, as a bevy of eggs the mothering wing
  Will, or mild nights the new morsels of spring:
Why, it seemed of course; seemed of right it should.

Lovely the woods, waters, meadows, combes, vales,
All the air things wear that build this world of Wales;
  Only the inmate does not correspond:
God, lover of souls, swaying considerate scales,
Complete thy creature dear O where it fails,
  Being mighty a master, being a father and fond.

Gerard Manley Hopkins

TEMPER IN OCTOBER

He rode at furious speed to Broken Edge,
And he was very angry, very small;
But God was kind, knowing he needed not
A scolding, nor a swift unpleasant fall,
Nor any high reproach of soul at all.
'It matters not,' said Reason and Good Sense;
'Absurd to let a trifle grow immense.'
'It matters very much,' said Busy Brain;
'You cannot be content and calm again,
For you are angry in a righteous cause.'
'Poor, queer old Waxy!' laughed the hips and haws.
'God has a sense of humour,' said a ball
Of orange-gold inside a spindle-berry—
'And "Christ our Lorde is full exceeding merrie." '

He lingered in the lane at Broken Edge,
Bryony berries burned from every hedge;
Snails in the deep wet grass of fairy rings
Told him of unimaginable things.
Love was in the colours of the sky,
Love in the folded shadows of the high
Blue hills, as quiet as any Easter Eve.
(O fool, O blind and earthbound thus to grieve!)

He turned his horse. Through level sunset-gleams
He saw a sudden little road that curled
And climbed elusive to a sky of dreams.
His anger over Broken Edge was hurled
To scatter into nothing on a gust
Of wind which brought the twilight to the trees.
The drifted leaves, the white October dust
Hiding the beechnuts for the squirrels' store,
Heard the low whisper spoken on his knees:—
'God, You have made a perfect world,
Don't let me spoil it ever any more.'

V. L. Edminson

A CAVE

. . . I discover, at the grotto's rear, another,
Even vaster cavern than the first. Here
The torrent has sought a deeper level,
Leaving only dry stones, that were once its bed
And stillness.

It is a stillness like something you can touch.
It is a terrible arch of silence, under which
My small heart smothers
Its pindrop beat.

Soundlessness.

I hold my breath,
And sit very still.

Soundlessness.

Memory is lost, and feeling
Numbed, in this elemental dumbness.
Even my faintest breathing sounds too loud.
The touch
Of hand to throat, or hand

On sleeve, however light, becomes
Too gross a noise.

Soundlessness.

A glass insect
Tinkles, I hear
The transparent ant's
Footfalls in the snows
Of soundlessness,
But so almost-soundlessly,
It is a whispered singing
In my own listening blood.

I sense the movement of
A single hair, that dries
With a hush, and shifts
Upon my forehead with
The sandy rustle of a single wave.

Inside the furry cavern of my ear,
A grain of earth
Is loosened, and tumbles like
An avalanche, so
Suddenly begun, so swiftly stilled,
As at the finish
All things begin
To come to this
Soundlessness;

And in the rushing universes
There shall be this
Stillness,
This motionless and grave serenity,
This perfect peace, the purest,
Most perpetual of motions,
A vast centre everywhere,
Forever soundless,
And forever still . . .

James Kirkup

BY FERRY TO THE ISLAND

We crossed by ferry to the bare island
where sheep and cows stared coldly through the
     wind—
the sea behind us with its silver water,
the silent ferryman standing in the stern
clutching his coat about him like old iron.

We landed from the ferry and went inland
past a small church down to the winding shore
where a white seagull fallen from the failing
chill and ancient daylight lay so pure
and softly breasted that it made more dear

the lesser white around us. There we sat
sheltered by a rock beside the sea.
Someone made coffee, someone played the fool
in a high rising voice for two hours.
The sea's language was more grave and harsh.

And one sat there whose dress was white and cool.
The fool sparkled his wit that she might hear
new diamonds turning on her naked finger.
What might the sea think or the dull sheep
lifting its head through heavy Sunday sleep?

And later, going home, a moon rising
at the end of a cart-track, minimum of red,
the wind being dark, imperfect cows staring
out of their half-intelligence, and a plough
lying on its side in the cold, raw

naked twilight, there began to move
slowly, like heavy water, in the heart
the image of the gull and of that dress,
both being white and out of the darkness rising
the moon ahead of us with its rusty ring.

                         Iain Crichton Smith

WE LYING BY SEASAND

We lying by seasand, watching yellow
And the grave sea, mock who deride
Who follow the red rivers, hollow
Alcove of words out of cicada shade,
For in this yellow grave of sand and sea
A calling for colour calls with the wind
That's grave and gay as grave and sea
Sleeping on either hand.
The lunar silences, the silent tide
Lapping the still canals, the dry tide-master
Ribbed between desert and water storm,
Should cure our ills of the water
With a one-coloured calm;
The heavenly music over the sand
Sounds with the grains as they hurry
Hiding the golden mountains and mansions
Of the grave, gay, seaside land.
Bound by a sovereign strip, we lie,
Watch yellow, wish for wind to blow away
The strata of the shore and drown red rock;
But wishes breed not, neither
Can we fend off rock arrival,
Lie watching yellow until the golden weather
Breaks, O my heart's blood, like a heart and hill.

Dylan Thomas

Part II

SERENE PEOPLE

INNOCENCE

How sweet is the shepherd's sweet lot!
From the morn to the evening he strays;
He shall follow his sheep all the day,
And his tongue shall be filled with praise.

For he hears the lambs innocent call,
And he hears the ewes tender reply;
He is watchful while they are in peace,
For they know when their shepherd is nigh,

William Blake

PLOUGHMAN SINGING

Here morning in the ploughman's songs is met
   Ere yet one footstep shows in all the sky,
And twilight in the east, a doubt as yet,
   Shows not her sleeve of grey to know her by.
Woke early, I arose and thought that first
   In winter-time of all the world was I.
The old owls might have hallooed if they durst,
   But joy just then was up and whistled by
A merry tune which I had known full long,
   But could not to my memory wake it back,
Until the ploughman changed it to the song.
   O happiness, how simple is thy track!
—Tinged like the willow shoots, the east's young brow
Glows red and finds thee singing at the plough.

John Clare

A SKETCH

The little hedge-row birds,
That peck along the road, regard him not.
He travels on, and in his face, his step,
His gait, is one expression; every limb,
His look and bending figure, all bespeak
A man who does not move with pain, but moves
With thought. He is insensibly subdued
To settled quiet: he is one by whom
All effort seems forgotten; one to whom
Long patience hath such mild composure given,
That patience now doth seem a thing of which
He hath no need. He is by Nature led
To peace so perfect, that the young behold
With envy what the old man hardly feels.

William Wordsworth

THE GARDENER

I took money and bought flowering trees
And planted them out on the bank to the east of
   the Keep.
I simply bought whatever had most blooms,
Not caring whether peach, apricot, or plum.
A hundred fruits, all mixed up together;
A thousand branches, flowering in due rotation.
Each has its season coming early or late;
But to all alike the fertile soil is kind.
The red flowers hang like a heavy mist;
The white flowers gleam like a fall of snow.
The wandering bees cannot bear to leave them;
The sweet birds also come there to roost.
In front there flows an ever-running stream;
Beneath there is built a little flat terrace.
Sometimes I sweep the flagstones of the terrace;
Sometimes, in the wind, I raise my cup and drink.
The flower-branches screen my head from the sun;

The flower-buds fall down into my lap.
Alone drinking, alone singing my songs,
I do not notice that the moon is level with the steps.
The people of Pa do not care for flowers;
All the spring no one has come to look.
But their Governor-General, alone with his cup of wine,
Sits till evening, and will not move from the place!

Po-Chü-I. Translated by Arthur Waley

EDDI'S SERVICE

(A.D. 687)

Eddi, priest of St. Wilfrid
   In his chapel at Manhood End,
Ordered a midnight service
   For such as cared to attend.

But the Saxons were keeping Christmas,
   And the night was stormy as well.
Nobody came to the service,
   Though Eddi rang the bell.

'Wicked weather for walking,'
   Said Eddi of Manhood End.
'But I must go on with the service
   For such as care to attend.'

The altar-lamps were lighted,—
   An old marsh-donkey came,
Bold as a guest invited,
   And stared at the guttering flame.

The storm beat on at the windows,
   The water splashed on the floor,
And a wet, yoke-weary bullock
   Pushed in through the open door.

'How do I know what is greatest,

How do I know what is least?
That is My Father's business,'
    Said Eddi, Wilfrid's priest.

But—three are gathered together—
    Listen to me and attend.
I bring good news, my brethren!'
    Said Eddi of Manhood End.

And he told the Ox of a Manger
    And a Stall in Bethlehem,
And he spoke to the Ass of a Rider,
    That rode to Jerusalem.

They steamed and dripped in the chancel,
    They listened and never stirred,
While, just as though they were Bishops,
    Eddi preached them The Word,

Till the gale blew off on the marshes
    And the windows showed the day,
And the Ox and the Ass together
    Wheeled and clattered away.

And when the Saxons mocked him,
    Said Eddi of Manhood End,
'I dare not shut His chapel
    On such as care to attend.'

Rudyard Kipling

THE GOOD PARSON

The parson of a country town was he
Who knew the straits of humble poverty;
But rich he was in holy thought and work,
Nor less in learning as became a clerk.
The word of Christ most truly did he preach,
And his parishioners devoutly teach.
Benign he was, in labors diligent,

And in adversity was still content—
As proved full oft. To all his flock a friend,
Averse was he to ban or to contend
When tithes were due. Much rather was he fond
Unto his poor parishioners around,
Of his own substance and his dues to give,
Content on little, for himself to live.
Wide was his parish, scattered far asunder,
Yet none did he neglect, in rain, or thunder.
Sorrow and sickness won his kindly care;
With staff in hand he travelled everywhere.
This good example to his sheep he brought
That first he wrought, and afterwards he taught
This parable he joined the Word unto—
That, 'If gold rust, what shall iron do?'
For if a priest be foul in whom we trust,
No wonder if a common man should rust!
And shame it were, in those the flock who keep
For shepherds to be foul yet clean the sheep.
Well ought a priest example fair to give,
By his own cleanness, how his sheep should live.
He did not put his benefice to hire,
And leave his sheep encumbered in the mire,
Then haste to St. Pauls in London Town,
To seek a chantry where to settle down,
And there at least to sing the daily mass,
Or with a brotherhood his time to pass.
He dwelt at home, with watchful care to keep
From prowling wolves his well-protected sheep.
Though holy in himself and virtuous
He still to sinful men was piteous,
Not sparing of his speech, in vain conceit,
But in his teaching kindly and discreet.
To draw his flock to heaven with noble art,
By good example, was his holy art.
Nor less did he rebuke the obstinate,
For pomp and worldly show he did not care,
No morbid conscience made his rule severe.
The lore of Christ and his apostles twelve
He taught, but first he followed it himself.

Geoffrey Chaucer

THE COUNTRY CLERGY

I see them working in old rectories
    By the sun's light, by candlelight,
Venerable men, their black cloth
A little dusty, a little green
With holy mildew. And yet their skulls,
Ripening over so many prayers,
Toppled into the same grave
With oafs and yokels. They left no books,
Memorial to their lonely thought
In grey parishes; rather they wrote
On men's hearts and in the minds
Of young children sublime words
Too soon forgotten. God in his time
Or out of time will correct this.

                                    R. S. Thomas

The man of life upright,
    Whose guiltless heart is free
From all dishonest deeds
    Or thought of vanity:

The man whose silent days
    In harmless joys are spent
Whom hopes cannot delude,
    Nor sorrow discontent:

That man needs neither towers
    Nor armour for defence,
Nor secret vaults to fly
    From thunder's violence.

He only can behold
    With unaffrighted eyes
The horrors of the deep
    And terrors of the skies.

Thus scorning all the cares
    That fate or fortune brings,
He makes the heaven his book,
    His wisdom heavenly things,

Good thoughts his only friends,
    His wealth a well-spent age,
The earth his sober inn
    And quiet pilgrimage.

Thomas Campion

ODE ON SOLITUDE

Happy the man whose wish and care
    A few paternal acres bound,
Content to breathe his native air,
      In his own ground.
Whose herds with milk, whose fields with bread,
    Whose flocks supply him with attire,
Whose trees in summer yield him shade,
      In winter fire.
Blest, who can unconcern'dly find
    Hours, days, and years slide soft away,
In health of body, peace of mind,
      Quiet by day,
Sound sleep by night; study and ease,
    Together mixt; sweet recreation;
And Innocence, which most does please
      With meditation.
Thus let me live, unseen, unknown,
    Thus unlamented let me die,
Steal from the world, and not a stone
      Tell where I lie.

Alexander Pope

A RECLUSE

Here lies (where all at peace may be)
A lover of mere privacy.
Graces and gifts were his; now none
Will keep him from oblivion;
How well they served his hidden ends
Ask those who knew him best, his friends.

He is dead; but even among the quick
This world was never his candlestick.
He envied none; he was content
With self-inflicted banishment.
'Let your light shine!' was never his way:
What then remains, Welladay!

And yet his very silence proved
How much he valued what he loved.
There peered from his hazed, hazel eyes
A self in solitude made wise;
As if within the heart may be
All the soul needs for company:
And, having that in safety there,
Finds its reflection everywhere.

Life's tempests must have waxed and waned:
The deep beneath at peace remained.
Full tides that silent well may be
Mark of no less profound a sea.
Age proved his blessing. It had given
The all that earth implies of heaven;
And found an old man reconciled
To die, as he had lived, a child.

Walter de la Mare

THE OLD MAN'S WISH

If I live to be old, for I find I go down,
Let this be my Fate in a country Town;
May I have a Warm House with a Stone at the Gate,
And a cleanly young Girl to rub my bald Pate.
  May I govern my Passion with an absolute sway,
  And grow wiser and better as my strength wears away;
  Without Gout or Stone by a gentle Decay.

In a Country Town by a murmuring Brook,
With the Ocean at distance on which I may look;
With a spacious Plain, without Hedge or Stile,
And an easie Pad nag to ride out a Mile.
  May I govern my Passion with an absolute sway,
  And grow wiser and better as my strength wears away;
  Without Gout or Stone by a gentle Decay.

With *Horace* and *Plutarch*, and one or two more,
Of the best Wits that liv'd in the Ages before;
With a dish of Roast Mutton, not Venison nor Teal,
And clean, though coarse, Linnen at every Meal.
  May I govern my Passion with an absolute sway,
  And grow wiser and better as my strength wears away;
  Without Gout or Stone by a gentle Decay.

With a Pudding on *Sunday*, and stout humming Liquor,
And remnants of Latin to welcome the Vicar;
With a hidden Reserve of *Burgundy* Wine,
To drink the King's Health in as oft as I dine.
  May I govern my Passion with an absolute sway,
  And grow wiser and better as my strength wears away;
  Without Gout or Stone by a gentle Decay.

With a Courage undaunted may I face the last day,
And when I am dead, may the better sort say,
(In the Morning when sober, in the Evening when Mellow)
He's gone, and leaves not behind him his Fellow.
  May I govern my Passion with an absolute sway,
  And grow wiser and better as my strength wears away;
  Without Gout or Stone by a gentle Decay.

Walter Pope

THE CALLS

A dismal fog-hoarse siren howls at dawn.
I watch the man it calls for, pushed and drawn
Backwards and forwards, helpless as a pawn.
    But I'm lazy, and his work's crazy.

Quick treble bells begin at nine o'clock,
Scuttling the schoolboy pulling up his sock,
Scaring the late girl in her inky frock.
    I must be crazy; I learn from the daisy.

Stern bells annoy the rooks and doves at ten.
I watch the verger close the doors, and when
I hear the organ moan the first amen,
    Sing my religions—same as pigeons.

A blatant bugle tears my afternoons.
Out clump the clumsy Tommies by platoons,
Trying to keep in step with rag-time tunes,
    But I sit still; I've done my drill.

Wilfred Owen

TWO CHARMS TO RESTORE LOST SERENITY

(i)

A CHARM FOR THE EAR-ACHE

Now let music, light as an enchanter's hands,
And warm and fragrant as a summer's air
Be gently breathed into this anxious ear.
Then, like a magic ointment, or fine sands
Of coral drowsed by an ocean's golden suns,
Let all wild sounds in quiet poems come
To charm the angry drum with murmured monotones.
Now let the face of love lift from a dream
His gravely smiling lips, and silent lay
Their honeyed wisdom here! O, let the tongue
With healing science harmonise my long
Discordances, and kiss all wakefulness at last away!

James Kirkup

A CHARM AGAINST THE TOOTHACHE

Venerable Mother Toothache
Climb down from the white battlements,
Stop twisting in your yellow fingers
The fourfold rope of nerves;
And tomorrow I will give you a tot of whisky
To hold in your cupped hands,
A garland of anise-flowers,
And three cloves like nails.

And tell the attendant gnomes
It is time to knock off now,
To shoulder their little pick-axes,
Their cold-chisels and drills.
And you may mount by a silver ladder
Into the sky, to grind
In the cracked polished mortar
Of the hollow moon.

By the lapse of warm waters,
And the poppies nodding like red coals,
The paths on the granite mountains,
And the plantation of my dreams.

John Heath-Stubbs

THE SOLITARY REAPER

Behold her, single in the field,
Yon solitary Highland lass!
Reaping and singing by herself.
Stop her, or gently pass!
Alone she cuts and binds the grain,
And sings a melancholy strain.
Oh, listen! for the vale profound
Is overflowing with the sound.

No nightingale did ever chant
So sweetly to reposing bands
Of travellers in some shady haunt
Among Arabian sands:
No sweeter voice was ever heard
In spring-time from the cuckoo-bird
Breaking the silence of the seas
Among the farthest Hebrides.

Will no one tell me what she sings?
Perhaps the plaintive numbers flow
For old, unhappy, far-off things,
And battles long ago:
Or is it some more humble lay,
Familiar matter of to-day?
Some natural sorrow, loss, or pain,
That has been, and may be again?

Whate'er the theme, the maiden sang
As if her song could have no ending;
I saw her singing at her work,
And o'er the sickle bending:—
I listen'd till I had my fill:
And, as I mounted by the hill,
The music in my heart I bore,
Long after it was heard no more.

William Wordsworth

FARM WIFE

Hers is the clean apron, good for fire
Or lamp to embroider, as we talk slowly
In the long kitchen, while the white dough
Turns to pastry in the great oven,
Sweetly and surely as hay making
In a June meadow; hers are the hands,
Humble with milking, but still now
In her wide lap as though they heard

A quiet music, hers being the voice
That coaxes time back to the shadows
In the room's corners. O, hers is all
This strong body, the safe island
Where men may come, sons and lovers,
Daring the cold seas of her eyes.

R. S. Thomas

A CHANT

With all our mirth, I doubt if we shall be
Like Martha here, in her serenity,
When we're her age; who goes from bed to bed
To wash the faces of the newly dead;
To close their staring eyes and comb their hair,
To cross their hands and change the linen there;
Who helps the midwives to give strength and breath
To babes, by almost beating them to death
With a wet towel; and half drowns them too,
Until their tender flesh is black and blue.
Not all the revels, Martha, we have been to
Can give us, when we're old, a peace like yours—
Due to the corpses you have gone and seen to.

W. H. Davies

ALMSWOMAN

At Quincey's moat the squandering village ends,
And there in the alms-house dwell the dearest friends
Of all the village, two old dames that cling
As close as any true-loves in the spring.
Long, long ago they passed three-score-and-ten,
And in this doll's house lived together then;
All things they have in common being so poor,
And their one fear, Death's shadow at the door.
Each sundown makes them mournful, each sunrise
Brings back the brightness in their failing eyes.

How happy go the rich fair-weather days
When on the roadside folk stare in amaze
At such a honeycomb of fruit and flowers
As mellows round their threshold; what long hours
They gloat upon their steepling hollyhocks,
Bee's balsams, feathery southernwood and stocks,
Fiery dragon's-mouths, great mallow leaves
For salves and lemon-plants in bushy sheaves,
Shagged Esau's-hands with five green finger-tips.
Such old sweet names are ever on their lips.

As pleased as little children where these grow
In cobbled pattens and worn gowns they go,
Proud of their wisdom when on gooseberry shoots
They stuck egg shells to fright from coming fruits
The brisk-billed rascals; scanning still to see
Their neighbour owls saunter from tree to tree,
Or in the hushing half-light mouse the lane
Long-winged and lordly.
                        But when those hours wane
Indoors they ponder, scared by the harsh storm
Whose pelting saracens on the window swarm,
And listen for the mail to clatter past
And church-clock's deep bay withering on the blast;
They feed the fire that flings its freakish light
On pictured kings and queens grotesquely bright,
Platters and pitchers, faded calendars
And graceful hour-glass trim with lavenders.

Many a time they kiss and cry and pray
That both be summoned in the selfsame day,
And wiseman linnet tinkling in his cage
End too with them the friendship of old age,
And all together leave their treasured room
Some bell-like evening when the May's in bloom.

                                        Edmund Blunden

TO AN OLD LADY ASLEEP AT A POETRY READING

Snore on in your front-row chair! Let not my voice
Disturb the wordless heaven that your eyes have found!
I, too, would welcome that release,
Here in this hard hall with the naked lights
In which my spirit and my words are bound,
The nightmare setting of all sleepless nights.

Why do the others, too, not briefly doze?
My voice has laid a healthy spell
Upon your gentle fret, and on a mind that glows
Still with a small but vivid fire.
They surely felt the moderate enchantment just as well?
Why do we all not sleep, abandoning these platforms that do
    more than tire?

Dear lady, do not let that wakeful vulture,
Your tiresome neighbour, provoke you with her nudging gloom.
She is one of those restless seekers after culture,
Guardians of Beauty who at Question-time will always shout
    for it,
While I desire only the chilly sanctuary of the chairman's
    guestroom.
Let her be on everything: you're better out of it!

Poor dear, she's wakened you. The sweet sleep sours.
Snug in your old fur-coat, you stare
Perplexed a moment, from under your hat's provincial flowers.
—You must not mind, old girl, as shame comes hunting you:
Try to preserve, as I do, this unruffled air . . .
Yes, dear, this is hell, and this is me confronting you.

James Kirkup

THE CAPTIVE

Not with an outcry to Allah nor any complaining
He answered his name at the muster and stood to the chaining.
When the twin anklets were nipped on the leg-bars that
    held them,
He brotherly greeted the armourers stooping to weld them.
Ere the sad dust of the marshalled feet of the chain-gang
    swallowed him,
Observing him nobly at ease, I alighted and followed him.
Thus we had speech by the way, but not touching his sorrow—
Rather his red Yesterday and his regal Tomorrow,

Wherein he statelily moved to the clink of his chains
    unregarded,
Nowise abashed but contented to drink of the potion awarded.
Saluting aloofly his Fate, he made haste with his story,
And the words of his mouth were as slaves spreading carpets
    of glory
Embroidered with names of the Djinns—a miraculous
    weaving—
But the cool and perspicuous eye overbore unbelieving.
So I submitted myself to the limits of rapture—
Bound by this man we had bound, amid captives his capture—
Till he returned me to earth and the vision departed.
But on him be the Peace and the Blessing: for he was
    great-hearted!

Rudyard Kipling

GUNGA DIN

You may talk o' gin and beer
When you're quartered safe out 'ere,
An' you're sent to penny-fights an' Aldershot it;
But when it comes to slaughter
You will do your work on water,
An' you'll lick the bloomin' boots of 'im that's got it.
Now in Injia's sunny clime.

Where I used to spend my time
A-servin' of 'Er Majesty the Queen,
Of all them blackfaced crew
The finest man I knew
Was our regimental bhisti, Gunga Din!
            He was 'Din! Din! Din!
  'You limpin' lump o' brick-dust, Gunga Din!
      'Hi! Slippy *hitherao*!
      'Water, get it! *Panee lao*[1]
  'You squidgy-nosed old idol, Gunga Din.'

The uniform 'e wore
Was nothin' much before,
An' rather less than 'arf o' that be'ind,
For a piece o' twisty rag
An' a goatskin water-bag
Was all the field-equipment 'e could find.
When the sweatin' troop-train lay
In a sidin' through the day,
Where the 'eat would make your bloomin' eyebrows crawl,
We shouted 'Harry By!'[2]
Till our throats were bricky-dry,
Then we wopped 'im 'cause 'e couldn't serve us all.
            It was 'Din! Din! Din!
  'You 'eathen, where the mischief 'ave you been?
      'You put some *juldee*[3] in it
      'Or I'll *marrow*[4] you this minute
  'If you don't fill my helmet, Gunga Din!'

'E would dot an' carry one
Till the longest day was done,
An' 'e didn't seem to know the use o' fear.
If we charged or broke or cut,
You could bet your bloomin' nut,
'E'd be waitin' fifty paces right flank rear.
With 'is mussick[5] on 'is back,

[1] Bring water swiftly.
[2] O brother.
[3] Be quick.
[4] Hit you.
[5] Water-skin.

'E would skip with our attack,
An' watch us till the bugles made 'Retire'
An' for all 'is dirty 'ide
'E was white, clear white, inside
When 'e went to tend the wounded under fire!
      It was 'Din! Din! Din!'
  With the bullets kickin' dust-spots on the green
      When the cartridges ran out,
        You could hear the front-ranks shout,
'Hi! ammunition-mules an' Gunga Din!'

I shan't forgit the night
When I dropped be'ind the fight
With a bullet where my belt-plate should a' been.
I was chokin' mad with thirst,
An' the man that spied me first
Was our good old grinnin', gruntin' Gunga Din.
'E lifted up my 'ead,
An' he plugged me where I bled,
An' e' guv me 'arf-a-pint o' water green.
It was crawlin' and it stunk,
But of all the drinks I've drunk,
I'm gratefullest to one from Gunga Din.
      It was 'Din! Din! Din!
  "Ere's a beggar with a bullet through 'is spleen;
     "E's chawin' up the ground,
     'An' 'e's kickin' all around:
'For Gawd's sake git the water, Gunga Din!'

'E carried me away
To where a dooli lay,
An' a bullet come an' drilled the beggar clean.
'E put me safe inside,
An' just before 'e died,
'I 'ope you liked your drink,' sez Gunga Din.
So I'll meet 'im later on
At the place where 'e is gone—
Where it's always double drill an' no canteen.
'E'll be squattin' on the coals
Givin' drinks to poor damned souls,
An' I'll get a swig in hell from Gunga Din!

Yes, Din! Din! Din!
You Lazarushian-leather Gunga Din!
Though I've belted you an' flayed you,
By the livin' Gawd that made you,
You're a better man than I am, Gunga Din!

                                        Rudyard Kipling

BUT MY NEIGHBOUR IS MY TREASURE

Solemn and lovely visions and holy dreams,
Mysterious portents, wanderers who range
Among unearthly themes,
Strong catalysts that change
The colour and the contours of the mind;
Be silent in your valleys in the moon,
Fade to the country that we never find:
For I am listening for that mortal tune,
The broken anthem of my fallen kind,
And seeking for the vision of those I see
Daily and here, in this poor house with me.

Their name is Wonderful, a holy name;
These in the light of heaven I shall behold,
If I can come there, standing in the flame
Of glory, with the blessed in their gold.
There is no dream more wonderful, for they
Are worth the whole creation, each alone.
Grant me to see their beauty on that Day!
There is no vision to prefer, but One.

Ruth Pitter

TO FRANZ KAFKA

If we, the proximate damned, presumptive blest,
Were called one day to some high consultation
With the authentic ones, the worst and best
Picked from all time, how mean would be our station.
Oh we could never bear the standing shame,
Equivocal ignominy of non-election;
We who will hardly answer to our name,
And on the road direct ignore direction.

But you, dear Franz, sad champion of the drab
And half, would watch the tell-tale shames drift in
(As if they were troves of treasure) not aloof,
But with a famishing passion quick to grab
Meaning, and read on all the leaves of sin
Eternity's secret script, the saving proof.

Edwin Muir

RENDEZVOUS WITH GOD

(The last stanzas of a poem describing the people of the world on the Day of Judgement. Each religious sect is sure that they alone are the favoured of God, and all have been too absorbed in the rituals of an exclusive Faith to remember Works. In the final reckoning only one man is found worthy to enter heaven.)

...There was one in the myriad throngs whom I chanced to know
A poor man by the standards of the word
Neglected for his lack of care, despised for his irreligion,
Who never was seen inside a mosque or temple or steeple-house
He did not belong to the Drepung, he knew no Tripitake,
Who read the Holy Books of God and Allah for amusement
And enjoyed them as poetry,
A dealer in heterodoxy; a reported heresiarch

He could only admire the architecture of cathedrals, go wild over arabesques
And mark the finesse of Jesse windows.
He loved domes; and gleefully clapped like little children
To see huge arches, and tall minarets.
With intense gratification, he watched the processions
Of Durga, of Our Lady of Fatima, and Muharram,
But none could point a finger at him with a charge of dishonesty,
None could impute baseness to his deeds.
Many blasphemies were ascribed to his authorship
'The time for prayers' he was wont to say, 'is after you have done one good deed.'
And so many heresies went after his name, as we relate
'Your Devotions and your Piety
Do not preclude, are not a guarantee
Against the evil in your hearts
Against the foulness in your arts
Since man being human cannot escape his mind of Herod,
But why tremble before your Master, why shake before your Lord?
When a man is honest, he can face his God!'
He stood to-day unperturbed, unshaken, calm as always
His hands in his pockets he watched carelessly
The trembling, ardent, suffering crowd near him
And smoked his tobacco as in the company of fools.
Then the moment of appointment came, earth and its mounds receded from sight
The stars and planets stepped aside and thunders reverberated in heavens,
He looked up—and looked back dauntlessly at a smiling God;
Saluted, strutted away to the paths of Paradise, accompanied by the angels of God
On that day of appointment, at the rendezvous with God.
And the crowd neither saw him move in light, nor saw this interview with God
They sweated, perspired, waited, terror-shaken, hope-benumbed, perdition-haunted
Expectant, ready, alert, aghast, bewildered, lost, forsaken, forgotten in the labyrinths

Of heavens whose chart they did not know, whose ways
they could not know
On that day of appointment, at the rendezvous with God
Mehdi Ali Seljouk

Part III

THEIR PEACEFUL WORK

ELEGY IN A MUSEUM

Such happiness—and all amongst the dead.
Bowls, jars and dishes hands fallen to shadows
Shaped lovingly and never knew how long
Their vision lay embalmed. Necklets and trinkets
Lay against glowing skin in flowering Greece,
Cherished and fingered—now coolly regarded
As our eyes skim them.
                        Slabs of broken friezes
Tumbled aloft from soaring pillars, dazzling
White against blue, in Greece, in ancient summers.

Our happiness was living and so passing,
And theirs was dead and safely stored forever.
How quiet their hearts, their golden day complete;
And ours, restless, envied them their cold treasure,
Wishing our present pain could be resolved
By time into such safe serenity.

Pamela Griffin

THE IMAGE-MAKER

Hard is the stone, but harder still
The delicate performing will
That, guided by a dream alone,
Subdues and moulds the hardest stone,
Making the stubborn jade release
The emblem of eternal peace.

If but the will be firmly bent,
No stuff resists the mind's intent;
The adamant abets his skill
And sternly aids the artist's will,
To clothe in perdurable pride
Beauty his transient eyes descried.

Oliver St. John Gogarty

HOLIDAYS IN CHILDHOOD

Last year Harold was making a boat
For his small cousin from the north country.
His tools and timber were not very good,
But he had clever fingers, the youth Harold,
And he had shaped the hull with all his skill,
Given it narrow lines to slip through water,
And cut the keel to give a seabird's poise.
The hull was finished, mast and bowsprit fitted,
Waiting for halyards, blocks, sails fore and aft
To change the shaven wood into a yacht.
It was going to be a trim and speedy ship.

The hull is in the outhouse now,
With the thick knife beside it.
It still looks like a swift and sturdy vessel,
And its prow seems eager for the waves.
The mountain still looms distantly beyond the town,
With the sky above it, and the strong winds
Whistling in the grasses as they always whistle.
The shops and houses are all just the same,
And the trams rattle by as they did last year—
Though this year Harold is dead.

Clifford Dyment

RETORT TO THE ANTI-ABSTRACTIONISTS

The world had grown too complicated, so
He went back to the cause of things and laid
The fiery day within an early shade.
It was impossible to see things grow.

And this he knew and meant. Do not believe
This picture was achieved without much care.
The man drew dangerously toward despair,
Trying to show what inward eyes perceive.

The pattern now demands our firm attention,
But still spectators say, 'What does it mean?
This is not anything I have seen.'
There is so much the painter could not mention.

His picture shows the meaning, not the thing—
The look without the face, flight without wings.

Elizabeth Jennings

HOMAGE TO J. S. BACH

It is good just to think about Johann Sebastian
Bach, grinding away like the mills of God,
Producing masterpieces, and legitimate children—
Twenty-one in all,—and earning his bread

Instructing choirboys to sing their UT, RE, MI,
Provincial and obscure. When Fame's trumpets told
Of Handel displaying magnificent wings of melody,
Setting the waters of Thames on fire with gold,

Old Bach's music did not seem to the point.
He groped in the Gothic vaults of polyphony,
Labouring pedantic miracles of counterpoint.
They did not know that the order of eternity

Transfiguring the order of the Age of Reason,
The timeless accents of super-celestial harmonies,
Filtered into time through that stupendous brain.
It was the dancing angels in their hierarchies,

Teaching at the heart of Reason that Passion existed,
And at the heart of Passion a Crucifixion,
When the great waves of his SANCTUS lifted
The blind art of music into a blinding vision.

John Heath-Stubbs

SHAKESPEARE

Others abide our question. Thou art free.
We ask and ask—Thou smilest and art still,
Out-topping knowledge. For the loftiest hill,
Who to the stars uncrowns his majesty,

Planting his steadfast footsteps in the sea,
Making the heaven of heavens his dwelling-place,
Spares but the cloudy border of his base
To the foil'd searching of mortality;

And thou, who didst the stars and sunbeams know,
Self-school'd, self-scann'd, self-honour'd, self-secure,
Didst tread on earth unguess'd at.—Better so!

All pains the immortal spirit must endure,
All weakness which impairs, all griefs which bow,
Find their sole speech in that victorious brow.

Matthew Arnold

SAT EST SCRIPSISSE

(To E.G., with a collection of essays)

When You and I have wandered beyond
    the reach of call,
And all our Works immortal lie scattered on the
    Stall,
It may be some new Reader, in that remoter
    age,
Will find the present Volume and listless turn the
    page.
For him I speak these verses. And, sir (I say
    to him),
This Book you see before you,—this masterpiece
    of Whim,
Of Wisdom, Learning, Fancy (if you will, please,
    attend),—

Was written by its Author, who gave it to his
   Friend.

For they had worked together,—been Comrades
   of the Pen;
They had their points at issue, they differed now
   and then;
Both loved Song and Letters, and each had
   close at heart
The hopes, the aspirations, the 'dear delays' of
   Art.

And much they talked of Measures, and more
   they talked of Style,
Of Form and 'lucid Order', of 'labour of the
   File';
And he who wrote the writing, as sheet by sheet was
   penned
(This all was long ago, Sir!), would read it to
   his Friend.

They knew not, nor cared greatly, if they were
   spark or star;
They knew to move is somewhat, although the
   goal be far;
And larger light or lesser, this thing at least is
   clear,
They served the Muses truly,—their service was
   sincere.

This tattered page you see, sir, this page alone
   remains
(Yes,—fourpence is the lowest!) of all those
   pleasant pains;
And as for him that read it, and as for him that wrote,
No Golden Book enrolls them among its 'Names of
   Note.'

And yet they had their office. Though they to-
   day are passed,

They marched in that procession where is no first
　　or last;
Though cold is now their hoping, though they no
　　more aspire,
They too had once their ardour—they handed on
　　the fire.

Austin Dobson

ESPECIALLY WHEN THE OCTOBER WIND

(The Making of a Poem)

Especially when the October wind
With frosty fingers punishes my hair,
Caught by the crabbing sun I walk on fire
And cast a shadow crab upon the land,
By the sea's side, hearing the noise of birds,
Hearing the raven cough in winter sticks,
My busy heart who shudders as she talks
Sheds the syllabic blood and drains her words.

Shut, too, in a tower of words, I mark
On the horizon walking like the trees
The wordy shapes of women, and the rows
Of the star-gestured children in the park.
Some let me make you of the vowelled beeches,
Some of the oaken voices, from the roots
Of many a thorny shire tell you notes,
Some let me make you of the water's speeches.

Behind a pot of ferns the wagging clock
Tells me the hour's word, the neural meaning
Flies on the shafted disk, declaims the morning
And tells the windy weather in the cock.
Some let me make you of the meadow's signs;
The signal grass that tells me all I know
Breaks with the wormy winter through the eye.
Some let me tell you of the raven's sins.

Especially when the October wind
(Some let me make you of autumnal spells,
The spider-tongued, and the loud hill of Wales)
With fists of turnips punishes the land,
Some let me make you of the heartless words.
The heart is drained that, spelling in the scurry
Of chemic blood, warned of the coming fury.
By the sea's side hear the dark-vowelled birds.

Dylan Thomas

SONG OF A MAN WHO HAS COME THROUGH

Not I, not I, but the wind that blows through me!
A fine wind is blowing the new direction of Time.
If only I let it bear me, carry me, if only it carry me!
If only, most lovely of all, I yield myself and am borrowed
By the fine, fine wind that takes its course through the
        chaos of the world
Like a fine, an exquisite chisel, a wedge-blade inserted;
If only I am keen and hard like the sheer tip of a wedge
Driven by invisible blows,
The rock will split, we shall come at the wonder, we shall
        find the Hesperides.

Oh, for the wonder that bubbles into my soul,
I would be a good fountain, a good well-head,
Would blur no whisper, spoil no expression.

What is the knocking?
What is the knocking at the door in the night?
It is somebody wants to do us harm.

No, no, it is the three strange angels.
Admit them, admit them.

D. H. Lawrence

Part IV

PEACEFUL CREATURES

THE MASS OF THE GROVE

In a pleasant place today,
Mantled by fine green hazel,
I listened at day's dawning
To a skilful speckled thrush
Singing a polished stanza,
Smooth lessons and prophecies.
The essence of discretion,
Love's messenger journeyed long,
Coming from fair Carmarthen
At my golden girl's command,
Wordy, needing no password,
To this spot, to Nentyrch brook.
Morfudd it was who sent him,
That melodious child of May.

About him there were hangings,
Blossoms of May's precious boughs,
His chasuble (they seemed like)
Of the wind's (green mantles) wings.
All gold, by God Almighty,
Was the altar's canopy.

I heard in glowing language
A long, no faltering, chant,
No stumble, or mumble, that
Read gospel to the parish.
On a hill of ashtrees there
He raised a leafy wafer,
And a nightingale near by,
Beautiful, slim, sweet-spoken,
The brook's songstress, rang sanctus
To the welkin, clear her call.
The offering was lofted
To heaven above the grove,

Worship to God our Father,
A chalice of bliss and love.

Such liturgy contents me,
Bred of birches in fair woods.

Dafydd ap Gwilym

THE YELLOWHAMMER

When shall I see the white-thorn leaves agen
And yellowhammers gathering the dry bents
By the dyke side, on stilly moor or fen,
Feathered with love and nature's good intents?
Rude is the tent this architect invents,
Rural the place, with cart ruts by dyke side.

Dead grass, horse hair and downy-headed bents
Tied to dead thistles—she doth well provide,
Close to a hill of ants where cowslips bloom
And shed o'er meadows far their sweet perfume.
In early spring, when winds blow chilly cold,
The yellowhammer, trailing grass, will come
To fix a place, and choose an early home,
With yellow breast and head of solid gold.

John Clare

THE PETTICHAP'S NEST

Well! in my many walks I've rarely found
A place less likely for a bird to form
Its nest—close by the rut-gulled wagon-road,
And on the almost bare foot-trodden ground,
With scarce a clump of grass to keep it warm!
Where not a thistle spreads its spears abroad,
Or prickly bush, to shield it from harm's way;

And yet so snugly made, that none may spy
It out, save peradventure. You and I
had surely passed it in our walk to-day,
Had chance not led us by it!—Nay, e'en now,
Had not the old bird heard us trampling by
And fluttered out, we had not seen it lie,
Brown as the roadway side. Small bits of hay
Plucked from the old propt haystack's pleachy brow,
And withered leaves, make up its outward wall,
Which from the gnarled oak-dotterel yearly fall,
And in the old hedge-bottom rot away.
Built like an oven, through a little hole,
Scarcely admitting e'en two fingers in,
Hard to discern, the birds snug entrance win,
'Tis lined with feathers warm as silken stole,
Softer than seats of down for painless ease,
And full of eggs scarce bigger even than peas!
Here's one most delicate, with spots as small
As dust and of a faint and pinky red.
We'll let them be, and safety guard them well;
For fear's rude paths around are thickly spread,
And they are left to many dangerous ways.
A green grasshopper's jump might break the shells,
Yet lowing oxen pass them morn and night,
And restless sheep around them hourly stray;
And no grass springs but hungry horses bite,
That trample past them twenty times a day.
Yet, like a miracle, in safety's lap
They still abide unhurt, and out of sight.
Stop! here's the bird—that woodman at the gap
Frightened him from the hedge; 'tis olive-green.
Well! I declare it is the pettichap!
Not bigger than the wren, and seldom seen.
I've often found her nest in chance's way,
When I in pathless woods did idly roam;
But never did I dream until to-day
A spot like this would be her chosen home.

John Clare

THE NIGHTINGALE AND THE GLOW-WORM

A nightingale, that all day long
Had cheered the village with his song,
Nor yet at eve his note suspended
Nor yet when eventide was ended
Began to feel, as well he might,
The keen demands of appetite;
When, looking eagerly around,
He spied far off, upon the ground,
A something shining in the dark,
And knew the glow-worm by his spark;
So stooping down from hawthorn top,
He thought to put him in his crop.
The worm, aware of his intent,
Harangued him thus, right eloquent—
     'Did you admire my lamp,' quoth he,
'As much as I your minstrelsy,
You would abhor to do me wrong,
As much as I to spoil your song;
For 'twas the self-same Power divine
Taught you to sing and me to shine;
That you with music, I with light,
Might beautify, and cheer the night.'
     The songster heard his short oration,
And, warbling out his approbation,
Released him, as my story tells,
And found a supper somewhere else.
     Hence jarring sectaries may learn
Their real interest to discern;
That brother should not war with brother,
And worry and devour each other;
But shine and sing by sweet consent,
Till life's poor transient night is spent,
Respecting, in each other's case,
The gifts of nature and of grace.
     Those Christians best deserve the name
Who studiously make peace their aim;
Peace both the duty and the prize
Of him that creeps and him that flies.

William Cowper

THE REDWING

The winter clenched its fist
And knuckles numb with frost
Struck blind at the blinding snow.
It was hard for domestic creatures,
Cows, humans, and such, to get
Shelter and warmth and food.
And then the redwings came,
Birds of the open field,
The wood, the wild, only
Extremity makes them yield.

I must admit that never
Before that day when thaw
Bled red to white in the west
Had I seen a redwing, but there
Where ivy-berries offered
A last everlasting lost
Hope of life I held
A redwing in my hand,
Still warm, and was it dead?
It had toppled from a tree
Too weak too frail to fill
Its crop before the frost
Again asked for the cost
Of a winter dosshouse rest.
So I saw what it was like.

Never before had I seen
A redwing, now a hundred
Hopped through the shivering town
Unrecognised, unknown,
To most who saw them save
Simply as 'birds'. They came
As poets come among us,
Driven in from the wild
Not asking nor expecting
To be recognized for what
They are—if they are not
The usual thrush you can

Identify them as dead.
I held it in my hand,
I knew that it was dead,
But still I willed it to live
Not asking nor expecting
Many to understand
Why I must will it so.
But I know what a redwing is,
And I know how I know.

Patric Dickinson

ON A COLD DAY

My sacrament of wine and broken bread
　Is now prepared, and ready to be done;
The Tit shall hold a crust with both his feet,
　While, crumb by crumb, he picks it like a bone.
The Thrush, ashamed of his thin ribs, has blown
　His feathers out, to make himself look fat;
The Robin, with his back humped twice as high,
　For pity's sake—has crossed my threshold mat.
The Sparrow's here, the Finch and Jenny Wren,
　The wine is poured, the crumbs are white and small—
And when each little mouth has broken bread—
　Shall I not drink and bless then one and all?

W. H. Davies

THE KINGFISHER

It was the Rainbow gave thee birth,
　And left thee all her lovely hues;
And, as her mother's name was Tears,
　So runs it in my blood to choose
For haunts the lonely pools, and keep
In company with trees that weep.

Go you and, with such glorious hues,
    Live with proud Peacocks in green parks;
On lawns as smooth as shining glass,
    Let every feather show its marks;
Get thee on boughs and clap thy wings
Before the windows of proud kings.

Nay, lovely Bird, thou are not vain;
    Thou has no proud, ambitious mind;
I also love a quiet place
    That's green, away from all mankind;
A lonely pool, and let a tree
Sigh with her bosom over me.

                                        W. H. Davies

THE WILD SWANS AT COOLE

The trees are in their autumn beauty,
The woodland paths are dry,
Under the October twilight the water
Mirrors a still sky;
Upon the brimming water among the stones
Are nine-and-fifty swans.

The nineteenth autumn has come upon me
Since I first made my count;
I saw, before I had well finished,
All suddenly mount
And scatter wheeling in great broken rings
Upon their clamorous wings.

I have looked upon those brilliant creatures,
And now my heart is sore.
All's changed since I, hearing at twilight,
The first time on this shore,
The bell-beat of their wings above my head,
Trod with a lighter tread.

Unwearied still, lover by lover,
They paddle in the cold
Companionable streams or climb the air;
Their hearts have not grown old;
Passion or conquest, wander where they will,
Attend upon them still.

But now they drift on the still water,
Mysterious, beautiful;
Among what rushes will they build,
By what lake's edge or pool
Delight men's eyes when I awake some day
To find they have flown away?

W. B. Yeats

THE SWAN'S NEST

Remembering the swan upon her nest,
That loose, scattery heap of twigs and tattery branches,
Concealment scorned, perched proudly, that great wild nest
On its island, river-rushed, reed-green, a flourish . . .
                          Remembering
I see the swan, serenely curved, in peace
Guarding in exquisite immunity
Her treasure, lapped in love.
I see her mate, thrashing in water-wild fury,
Diamond-spattered beak scattering, tossing;
Arching an elegant neck in writhing aggression,
A guardian too . . .
                     And I lean on the bridge,
Hearing the river's dark, wintery gurgle,
Seeing the black leaves, the rigid branches,
Sensing ice in the wind's northern caverns,
Remembering a spring-dappling day,
Remembering the swan upon her nest.

Pamela Griffin

BIRD OF PARADISE

At sunset, only to his true love,
The bird of paradise opened wide his wings
Displaying emerald plumage shot with gold
Unguessed even by him.
                              True, that wide crest
Had blazoned royal estate, and the tropic flowers
Through which he flew had shown example
Of what brave colours gallantry might flaunt,
But these were other. She asked herself, trembling:
'What did I do to awake such glory?'

Robert Graves

STORK IN JEREZ

White-arched in loops of silence, the bodega
Lies drowsed in spices, where the antique woods
Oiled in solera, dripping years of flavour,
Distil their golden fumes among the shades.

In from the yard—where barrels under fig-trees
Split staves of sunlight from the noon's hot glare—
The tall stork comes; black-stilted, sagely witted,
Wiping his careful beak upon the air.

He is a priest-like presence, he inscribes
Sharp as a pen his staid and written dance,
Skating the floor with stiffened plumes behind him,
Gravely off-balance, solemn in his trance.

Drunk on these sherry vapours, eyes akimbo,
He treads among the casks, makes a small leap,
Flaps wildly, fails to fly—until at last
Folded umbrella-wise, he falls asleep.

So bird and bard exchange their sphere of pleasure:
He, from his high-roofed nest now levelled lies;
Whilst I, earth-tied, breathing these wines take wing
And float amazed across his feathered skies.

Laurie Lee

WILD BEES

These children of the sun which summer brings
As pastoral minstrels in her merry train
Pipe rustic ballads upon busy wings
And glad the cotters' quiet toils again.
The white-nosed bee that bores its little hole
In mortared walls and pipes its symphonies,
And never absent cousin, black as coal,
That Indian-like bepaints its little thighs,
With white and red bedight for holiday,
Right earlily a-morn do pipe and play
And with their legs stroke slumber from their eyes;
And aye so fond they of their singing seem
That in their holes abed at close of day
They still keep piping in their honey dreams;
And larger ones that thrum on ruder pipe
Round the sweet-smelling closen and rich woods,
Where tawny white and red-flusht clover buds
Shine bonnily, and bean-fields, blossom-ripe,
Shed dainty perfumes and give honey food
To these sweet poets of the summer fields;
Me much delighting as I stroll along
The narrow path that hay-laid meadow yields,
Catching the windings of their wandering song.
The black and yellow bumble, first on wing
To buzz among the sallow's early flowers,
Hiding its nest in holes from fickle spring
Who stints his rambles with her frequent showers;
And one that may for wiser piper pass,
In livery dress half sables and half red,
Who laps a moss-ball in the meadow grass
And hoards her stores when April showers have fled;
And russet commoner who knows the face
Of every blossom that the meadow brings,
Starting the traveller to a quicker pace
By threatening round his head in many rings:
These sweeten summer in their happy glee
By giving for her honey melody.

John Clare

THE CATERPILLAR

He crawleth here. He creypth there
  On lyttel cat-like feet.
He weareth coats of gorgeous fur
  And lyveth but to eat.

He gnaweth lettuce into shreddes
  And, burrowing with his nose,
He tattereth half the garden beddes
  And fretteth e'en the rose.

And yet his metaphysics lend
  The creature some renowne.
In him, a super-natural end
  Is Nature's natural crowne.

For, out of his own mouth at last
  He spinneth his cocoon
Wherein he swingeth, slumber-fast,
  Beneath the summer moon;

To dream, in silken hammock curled
  Of strange translunar things;
And wake, into a finer world,
  An Emperor, with wings.

Alfred Noyes

BUTTERFLIES

As butterflies are but winged flowers,
  Half sorry for their change, who fain,
So still and long they lie on leaves,
  Would be thought flowers again—

E'en so my thoughts, that should expand,
  And grow to higher themes above,
Return like butterflies to lie
  On the old things I love.

W. H. Davies

THE DRAGONFLY

Now, when my roses are half buds, half flowers,
   And loveliest, the king of flies has come—
It was a fleeting visit, all too brief;
   In three short minutes he had seen them all,
And rested, too, upon an apple leaf.

There, his round shoulders bumped with emeralds,
   A gorgeous opal crown set on his head,
And all those shining honours to his breast—
   'My garden is a lovely place,' thought I,
'But is it worthy of so fine a guest?'

He rested there upon that apple leaf—
   'See, see,' I cried amazed, 'his opal crown,
And all those emeralds clustered round his head!'
   'His breast, my dear, how lovely was his breast'—
The voice of my Beloved quickly said.

'See, see his gorgeous crown, that shines
   With all those jewels bulging round its rim'—
I cried aloud at night, in broken rest.
   Back came the answer quickly in my dream—
'His breast, my dear, how lovely was his breast!'

W. H. Davies

SHIV AND THE GRASSHOPPER

Shiv, who poured the harvest and made the winds to blow,
Sitting at the doorways of a day of long ago,
Gave to each his portion, food and toil and fate,
From the King upon the *guddee*[1] to the Beggar at the gate.
   All things made he—Shiva the Preserver.
   Mahadeo! Mahadeo! He made all,—
   Thorn for the camel, fodder for the kine,
   And Mother's heart for sleepy head, O little Son of mine!

[1] Throne.

Wheat he gave to rich folk, millet to the poor,
Broken scraps for holy men that beg from door to door;
Cattle to the tiger, carrion to the kite,
And rags and bones to wicked wolves without the wall at night.
Naught he found too lofty, none he saw too low—
Parbati beside him watched them come and go;
Thought to cheat her husband, turning Shiv to jest—
Stole the little grasshopper and hid it in her breast.
  So she tricked him, Shiva the Preserver.
  Mahadeo! Mahadeo, turn and see!
  Tall are the camels, heavy are the kine,
  But this was Least of Little Things, O little Son of mine!

When the dole was ended, laughingly she said,
'Master, of a million mouths is not one unfed?'
Laughing, Shiv made answer, 'All have had their part,
Even he, the little one, hidden 'neath thy heart.'
From her breast she plucked it, Parbati the thief,
Saw the Least of Little Things gnawed a new-grown leaf!
Saw and feared and wondered, making prayer to Shiv,
Who hath surely given meat to all that live!
  All things made he—Shiva the Preserver.
  Mahadeo! Mahadeo! He made all,—
  Thorn for the camel, fodder for the kine,
  And Mother's heart for sleepy head, O little Son of mine!

Rudyard Kipling

UPON THE SNAIL

She goes but softly, but she goeth sure;
She stumbles not as stronger creatures do:
Her journey's shorter, so she may endure
Better than they which do much further go.

She makes no noise, but stilly seizeth on
The flower or herb appointed for her food,
The which she quietly doth feed upon,
While others range, and gare, but find no good.

And though she doth but very softly go,
However 'tis not fast, nor slow, but sure;
And certainly they that do travel so,
The prize they do aim at, they do procure.

John Bunyan

MINNOWS

Linger awhile upon some bending planks
That lean against a streamlet's rushy banks,
And watch intently Nature's gentle doings:
They will be found softer than ring-dove's cooings.
How silent comes the water round that bend;
Not the minutest whisper does it send
To the o'erhanging sallows: blades of grass
Slowly across the chequer'd shadows pass.
Why, you might read two sonnets, ere they reach
To where the hurrying freshnesses aye preach
A natural sermon o'er their pebbly beds;
Where swarms of minnows show their little heads,
Staying their wavy bodies 'gainst the streams,
To taste the luxury of sunny beams
Temper'd with coolness. How they ever wrestle
With their own sweet delight, and ever nestle
Their silver bellies on the pebbly sand.
If you but scantily hold out the hand,
That very instant not one will remain;
But turn your eye, and they are there again.

John Keats

BABY TORTOISE

You know what it is to be born alone,
Baby tortoise!

The first day to heave your feet little by little from the shell,
Not yet awake,
And remain lapsed on earth,
Not quite alive.
A tiny, fragile, half-animate bean.

To open your tiny beak-mouth, that looks as if it would never
    open,
Like some iron door;
To lift the upper hawk-beak from the lower base
And reach your skinny little neck
And take your first bite at some dim bit of herbage,
Alone, small insect,
Tiny bright-eye,
Slow one.

To take your first solitary bite
And move on your slow, solitary hunt.
Your bright, dark little eye,
Your eye of a dark disturbed night,
Under its slow lid, tiny baby tortoise,
So indomitable.

No one ever heard you complain.

You draw your head forward, slowly, from your little wimple
And set forward, slow-dragging, on your four-pinned toes,
Rowing slowly forward.
Whither away, small bird?

Rather like a baby working its limbs,
Except that you make slow, ageless progress
And a baby makes none.

The touch of sun excites you,
And the long ages, and the lingering chill

Make you pause to yawn,
Opening your impervious mouth,
Suddenly beak-shaped, and very wide, like some suddenly
    gaping pincers;
Soft red tongue, and hard thin gums,
Then close the wedge of your little mountain front,
Your face, baby tortoise.

Do you wonder at the world, as slowly you turn your
    head in its wimple
And look with laconic, black eyes?
Or is sleep coming over you again,
The non-life?

You are so hard to wake.

Are you able to wonder?
Or is it just your indomitable will and pride of the first life
Looking round
And slowly pitching itself against the inertia
which had seemed invincible?

The vast inanimate,
And the fine brilliance of your so tiny eye,
Challenger.

Nay, tiny shell-bird
What a huge vast inanimate it is, that you must row against,
What an incalculable inertia.

Challenger,
Little Ulysses, fore-runner,
No bigger than my thumb-nail,
Buon viaggio.

All animate creation on your shoulder,
Set forth, little Titan, under your battle-shield.

The ponderous, preponderate,
Inanimate universe;
And you are slowly moving, pioneer, you alone.

How vivid your travelling seems now, in the troubled sunshine,
Stoic, Ulyssean atom;
Suddenly hasty, reckless, on high toes.
Voiceless little bird,
Resting your head half out of your wimple
In the slow dignity of your eternal pause.
Alone, with no sense of being alone,
And hence six times more solitary;
Fulfilled of the slow passion of pitching through immemorial
    ages
Your little round home in the midst of chaos.
Over the garden earth,
Small bird,
Over the edge of all things.

Traveller,
With your tail tucked a little on one side
Like a gentleman in a long-skirted coat.

All life carried on your shoulder,
Invincible fore-runner.

D. H. Lawrence

TORTOISE SHELL

The Cross, the Cross
Goes deeper in than we know,
Deeper into life;
Right into the marrow
And through the bone.

Along the back of the baby tortoise
The scales are locked in an arch like a bridge,
Scale-lapping, like a lobster's sections
Or a bee's.

Then crossways down his sides
Tiger-stripes and wasp-bands.

Five, and five again, and five again,
And round the edges twenty-five little ones,
The sections of the baby tortoise shell.
Four, and a keystone;
Four, and a keystone;
Four, and a keystone;
Then twenty-four, and a tiny little keystone.

It needed Pythagoras to see life playing with counters
        on the living back
Of the baby tortoise;
Life establishing the first eternal mathematical tablet,
Not in stone, like the Judean Lord, or bronze, but in
        life-clouded, life-rosy tortoise shell.
The first little mathematical gentleman
Stepping, wee mite, in his loose trousers
Under all the eternal dome of mathematical law.

Fives, and tens,
Threes and fours and twelves,
All the *volte face* of decimals,
The whirligig of dozens and the pinnacle of seven.

Turn him on his back,
The kicking little beetle,
And there again, on his shell-tender, earth-touching belly,
The long cleavage of division, upright of the eternal cross
And on either side count five,
On each side, two above, on each side, two below
The dark bar horizontal.

The Cross!
It goes right through him, the sprottling insect,
Through his cross-wise cloven psyche,
Through his five-fold complex-nature.

So turn him over on his toes again;
Four pin-point toes, and a problematical thumb-piece,
Four rowing limbs, and one wedge-balancing head,
Four and one makes five, which is the clue to all mathematics.

The Lord wrote it all down on the little slate
Of the baby tortoise.
Outward and visible indication of the plan within,
The complex, manifold involvedness of an individual creature
Plotted out
On this small bird, this pediment
Of all creation,
This slow one.

D. H. Lawrence

THE RAT

My windows now are giant drops of dew,
   The common stones are dancing in my eyes;
The light is winged, and panting, and the world
   Is fluttering with a little fall or rise.

See, while they shoot the sun with singing Larks,
   How those broad meadows sparkle and rejoice!
Where can the Cuckoo hide in all this light,
   And still remain unseen, and but a voice?

Shall I be mean, when all this light is mine?
   Is anything unworthy of its place?
Call for the rat, and let him share my joy,
   And sit beside me here, to wash his face.

W. H. Davies

SHEEP AND LAMBS

All in the April evening,
   April airs were abroad;
The sheep with their little lambs
   Passed me by on the road.

93

The sheep with their little lambs
    Passed me by on the road;
All in the April evening,
    I thought on the Lamb of God.

The lambs were weary, and crying
    With a weak, human cry.
I thought on the Lamb of God
    Going meekly to die.

Up in the blue, blue mountains
    Dewy pastures are sweet;
Rest for the little bodies,
    Rest for the little feet.

But for the Lamb of God
    Up on the hill-top green,
Only a Cross of shame,
    Two stark crosses between.

All in the April evening,
    April airs were abroad;
I saw the sheep with their lambs,
    And thought on the Lamb of God.

Katharine Tynan

THE OXEN

Christmas Eve, and twelve of the clock
    'Now they are all on their knees.'
An elder said as we sat in a flock
    By the embers in hearthside ease.

We pictured the meek mild creatures where
    They dwelt in their strawy pen,
Nor did it occur to one of us there
    To doubt they were kneeling then.

So fair a fancy few would weave
    In these years! Yet, I feel,
If someone said on Christmas Eve,
    'Come; see the oxen kneel

'In the lonely barton by yonder coomb
    Our childhood used to know,'
I should go with him in the gloom,
    Hoping it might be so.

Thomas Hardy

THE GOAT PATHS

The crooked paths go every way
    Upon the hill—they wind about
    Through the heather in and out
Of the quiet sunniness.
And there the goats, day after day,
    Stray in the sunny quietness,
Cropping here and cropping there,
    As they pause and turn and pass,
Now a bit of heather spray,
    Now a mouthful of grass.

In the deeper sunniness,
    In the place where nothing stirs,
Quietly in quietness,
    In the quiet of the furze,
For a time they come and lie
Staring on the roving sky.
If you approach they run away,
    They leap and stare, away they bound
    With a sudden angry sound.
To the sunny quietude:
    Crouching down where nothing stirs
    In the silence of the furze,
Crouching down again to brood
In the sunny solitude;

If I were as wise as they
I would stray apart and brood,
I would beat a hidden way
Through the quiet heather spray
And should you come I'd run away,
To a sunny solitude;
I would make an angry sound,
I would stare and turn and bound
To a deeper quietude,
To the place where nothing stirs
In the silence of the furze.
In that airy quietness
I would think as long as they;
Through the quiet sunniness
I would stray away to brood
By a hidden beaten way
In sunny solitude.

I would think until I found
Something I can never find,
Something lying on the ground,
In the bottom of my mind.

James Stephens

ON A HARE

Here lies, whom hound did ne'er pursue,
  Nor swifter greyhound follow,
Whose foot ne'er tainted morning dew,
  Nor ear heard huntsman's halloo;

Old Tiney, surliest of his kind,
  Who, nursed with tender care,
And to domestic bounds confined,
  Was still a wild Jack hare.

Though duly from my hand he took
  His pittance every night,
He did it with a jealous look,
  And, when he could, would bite.

His diet was of wheaten bread,
    And milk, and oats, and straw;
Thistles, or lettuces instead,
    With sand to scour his maw.

On twigs of hawthorn he regaled,
    On pippins' russet peel,
And, when his juicy salads failed,
    Sliced carrot pleased him well.

A Turkey carpet was his lawn,
    Whereon he loved to bound,
To skip and gambol like a fawn,
    And swing his rump around.

His frisking was at evening hours,
    For then he lost his fear,
But most before approaching showers,
    Or when a storm drew near.

Eight years and five round-rolling moons
    He thus saw steal away,
Dozing out all his idle noons,
    And every night at play.

I kept him for his humour's sake,
    For he would oft beguile
My heart of thoughts that made it ache,
    And force me to a smile.

But now beneath this walnut shade
    He finds his long last home,
And waits, in snug concealment laid,
    Till gentler Puss shall come.

He, still more aged, feels the shocks
    From which no care can save,
And, partner once of Tiney's box,
    Must soon partake his grave.

William Cowper

THE BADGER

Last of the night's quaint clan
  He goes his way—
A simple gentleman
  In sober grey;
To match lone paths of his
  In woodlands dim,
The moons of centuries
  Have silvered him.

Deep in the damp, fresh earth
  He roots and rolls,
And builds his winter girth
  Of sylvan tolls :
When seek the husbandmen
  The furrows brown,
He hies him to his den
  And lays him down.

There he may rest for me,
  Nor ever stir
For clamorous obloquy
  Of terrier;
Last of the night's quaint clan
  He curls in peace—
A friendly gentleman
  In grey pelisse!

P. R. Chalmers

THE ROAD SONG OF THE BANDAR LOG

Here we go in a flung festoon,
Half-way up to the jealous moon!
Don't you envy our pranceful bands?
Don't you wish you had extra hands?
Wouldn't you like if your tails were—so—
Curved in the shape of a Cupid's bow?

Now you're angry, but—never mind,
Brother, thy tail hangs down behind!

Here we sit in a branchy row,
Thinking of beautiful things we know;
Dreaming of deeds that we mean to do,
All complete, in a minute or two—
Something noble and grand and good,
Won by merely wishing we could.
Now we're going to—never mind,
Brother, thy tail hangs down behind!

All the talk we ever have heard
Uttered by bat or beast or bird—
Hide or fin or scale or feather—
Jabber it quickly and all together!
Excellent! Wonderful! Once again!
Now we are talking just like men.
Let's pretend we are . . . Never mind!
Brother, thy tail hangs down behind!
This is the way of the Monkey-kind!

Then join our leaping lines that scumfish through the pines,
That rocket by where, light and high, the wild-grape swings.
By the rubbish in our wake, and the noble noise we make,
Be sure—be sure, we're going to do some splendid things!

                                        Rudyard Kipling

MILK FOR THE CAT

When the tea is brought at five o'clock,
And all the neat curtains are drawn with care,
The little black cat with bright green eyes
Is suddenly purring there.

At first she pretends, having nothing to do,
She has come in merely to blink by the grate,
But, though tea may be late or the milk may be sour,
She is never late.

And presently her agate eyes
Take a soft large milky haze,
And her independent casual glance
Becomes a stiff, hard gaze.

Then she stamps her claw or lifts her ears,
Or twists her tail and begins to stir,
Till suddenly all her lithe body becomes
One breathing, trembling purr.

The children eat and wriggle and laugh;
The two old ladies stroke their silk:
But the cat is grown small and thin with desire,
Transformed to a creeping lust for milk.

The white saucer like some full moon descends
At last from the clouds of the table above;
She sighs and dreams and thrills and glows,
Transfigured with love.

She nestles over the shining rim,
Buries her chin in the creamy sea;
Her tail hangs loose; each drownsy paw
Is doubled under each bending knee.

A long, dim ecstasy holds her life:
Her world is an infinite shapeless white,
Till her tongue has curled the last holy drop,
Then she sinks back into the night,

Draws and dips her body to heap
Her sleepy nerves in the great arm-chair,
Lies defeated and buried deep
Three or four hours unconscious there.

Harold Monro

A SCHOLAR AND HIS DOG

I was a scholar; seven useful springs
Did I deflower in quotations
Of cross'd opinions 'bout the soul of man;
The more I learnt, the more I learnt to doubt.
Delight, my spaniel, slept, whilst I baused leaves,
Toss'd o'er the dunces, pored on the old print
Of titled words; and still my spaniel slept.
Whilst I wasted lamp-oil, baited my flesh,
Shrunk up my veins, and still my spaniel slept,
And still I held converse with Zabarell,
Aquinas, Scotus, and the musty saws
Still on went I: first, *an sit anima*;
Then, an 'twere mortal. O hold hold! at that
They're at brain buffets, fell by the ears, amain
(Pell-mell) together: still my spaniel slept.
Then, whether 'twere corporeal, local, fixt,
Ex traduce; but whether'd had free will
Or not, hot philosophers
Stood banding factions, all so strongly propt,
I staggered, knew not which was firmer part;
Stuffed noting-books: and still my spaniel slept.
At length he waked, and yawned: And by yon sky
For aught I know, he knew as much as I!

John Marston

THE PEACEMAKER

When she threatened to leave me,
    And I, full of evil,
Cried, 'Hoi, tiddleee, hoi,
    Here's work for the devil—'

With a sharp, single cry,
    With a quick, sudden burst,
Up sat our little blind dog,
    And begged to be nursed.

W. H. Davies

THE HORSES

I climbed through woods in the hour-before-dawn dark.
Evil air, a frost-making stillness,

Not a leaf, not a bird,—
A world cast in frost. I came out above the wood

Where my breath left tortuous statues in the iron light.
But the valleys were draining the darkness

Till the moorline—Blackening dregs of the brightening grey—
Halved the sky ahead. And I saw the horses:

Huge in the dense grey—ten together—
Megalith-still. They breathed, making no move,

With draped manes and tilted hind-hooves,
Making no sound.

I passed: not one snorted or jerked its head.
Grey silent fragments

Of a grey silent world.

I listened in emptiness on the moor-ridge.
The curlew's tear turned its edge on the silence.

Slowly detail leafed from the darkness. Then the sun
Orange, red, red erupted

Silently, and splitting to its core tore and flung cloud,
Shook the gulf open, showed blue,

And the big planets hanging—,
I turned

Stumbling in the fever of a dream, down towards
The dark woods, from the kindling tops,

And came to the horses. There, still they stood,

But now steaming and glistening under the flow of light,

Their draped stone manes, their tilted hind-hooves
Stirring under a thaw while all around them

The frost showed its fires. But still they made no sound.
Not one snorted or stamped,

Their hung heads patient as the horizons,
High over valleys, in the red levelling rays—

In din of the crowded streets, going among the years, the faces
May I still meet my memory in so lonely a place

Between the streams and the red clouds, hearing curlews,
Hearing the horizons endure.

Ted Hughes

THE HORSES

Barely a twelvemonth after
The seven days war that put the world to sleep,
Late in the evening the strange horses came.
By then we had made our covenant with silence,
But in the first few days it was so still
We listened to our breathing and were afraid.
On the second day
The radios failed; we turned the knobs; no answer.
On the third day a warship passed us, heading north,
Dead bodies piled on the deck. On the sixth day
A plane plunged over us into the sea. Thereafter
Nothing. The radios dumb;
And still they stand in corners of our kitchens,
And stand, perhaps, turned on, in a million rooms
All over the world. But now if they should speak,
We would not listen, we would not let it bring
That old bad world that swallowed its children quick
At one great gulp. We would not have it again.

Sometimes we think of the nations lying asleep,
Curled blindly in impenetrable sorrow,
And then the thought confounds us with its strangeness.
The tractors lie about our fields; at evening
They look like dank sea-monsters couched and waiting.
We leave them where they are and let them rust:
'They'll moulder away and be like other loam.'
We make our oxen drag our rusty ploughs,
Long laid aside. We have gone back
Far past our fathers' land.

                              And then, that evening
Late in the summer the strange horses came.
We heard a distant tapping on the road,
A deepening drumming; it stopped, went on again
And at the corner changed to hollow thunder.
We saw the heads
Like a wild wave charging and were afraid.
We had sold our horses in our fathers' time
To buy new tractors. Now they were strange to us
As fabulous steeds set on an ancient shield
Or illustrations in a book of knights.
We did not dare go near them. Yet they waited,
Stubborn and shy, as if they had been sent
By an old command to find our whereabouts
And that long-lost archaic companionship.
In the first moment we had never a thought
That they were creatures to be owned and used.
Among them were some half-dozen colts
Dropped in some wilderness of the broken world,
Yet new as if they had come from their own Eden.
Since then they have pulled our ploughs and borne our loads,
But that free servitude can pierce our hearts.
Our life is changed; their coming our beginning.

                                        Edwin Muir

'MAN IS A LUMPE WHERE ALL BEASTS KNEADED BE'

Is this your duty? Never lay your ear
Back to your skull and snarl, bright Tiger! Down
Bruin! Grimalkin back! Did you not hear
    Man's voice and see Man's frown?

Too long, sleek purring Panther, you have paid
Your flatteries, far too long about my breast
You, Snake, like Ivy have coiled. I'll not be stayed,
    I know my own way best.

Down, the whole pack! or else . . . so; now you are meek.
But then, alas, your eyes. Poor cowering brutes,
Your boundless pain, your strength to bear so weak—
    It bites at my heart-roots.

Oh, courage. I'll come back when I've grown shepherd
To feed you, and grown child to lead you all
Where there's green pasture waiting for the leopard
    And for the wolf a stall;

But not before I've come where I am bound
And made the end and the beginning meet,
When over and under Earth I have travelled round
    The whole heaven's milky street.

                   C. S. Lewis

The wolf also shall dwell with the lamb, and the leopard shall
lie down with the kid; and the calf and the young lion and the
fatling together; and a little child shall lead them.

And the cow and the bear shall feed; their young ones shall
lie down together: and the lion shall eat straw like the ox.

And the suckling child shall play on the hole of the asp, and
the weaned child shall put his hand on the cockatrice' den.

They shall not hurt nor destroy in all my holy mountain: for
the earth shall be full of the knowledge of the Lord, as the
waters cover the sea.

               Isaiah (Chapter XI v. 6-9)

Part V

PEACEFUL SIGHTS AND SOUNDS

UNDERSTANDING

To walk abroad is, not with eyes,
But thoughts, the fields to see and prize;
   Else may the silent feet,
     Like logs of wood,
Move up and down, and see no good,
   Nor joy nor glory meet.

Ev'n carts and wheels their place do change,
But cannot see, though very strange
   The glory that is by:
     Dead puppets may
Move in the bright and glorious day,
   Yet not behold the sky.

And are not men than they more blind,
Who having eyes yet never find
   The bliss in which they move?
     Like statues dead
They up and down are carried
   Yet neither see nor love.

To walk is by a thought to go,
To move in spirit to and fro,
   To mind the good we see,
     To taste the sweet,
Observing all the things we meet
   How choice and rich they be . . .

Thomas Traherne

THE STARS

Blessed be the Maker's name
By whose craft stars were fashioned,
For there is nothing brighter
Than the small, round, pure-white star.
The high heaven's light it is,
A clear and steady candle.
This candle will not grow dim,
And no deceit can steal it;
Fall winds will not blow it out,
Heaven's roof's holy wafer;
Flood waters will not drown it,
Woman on watch, dish of saints.
No robber's hands will reach it,
Base of the Trinity's bowl;
It's not proper for a man
To seek a pearl of Mary's.
It will light every region,
Coin of minted yellow gold.
It is the light's true buckler,
The shape of the sky's bright sun . . .
Christ on high will put it out,
And sand it, but not shortly,
Its shape like a round white loaf,
To sleep in the sky's shadow.

Dafydd ap Gwilym

Bright Star! would I were steadfast as thou art—
  Not in lone splendour hung aloft the night,
And watching, with eternal lids apart,
  Like Nature's patient, sleepless Eremite,
The moving waters at their priestlike task
  Of pure ablution round earth's human shores,
Or gazing on the new soft fallen mask
  Of snow upon the mountains and the moors—
No—yet still steadfast, still unchangeable.
  Pillow'd upon my fair love's ripening breast,

To feel for ever its soft fall and swell,
   Awake for ever in a sweet unrest,
Still, still to hear her tender-taken breath,
And so live ever—or else swoon to death.

John Keats

So in the empty sky the stars appear,
Are bright in heaven marching through the sky,
Spinning their planets, each one to his year,
Tossing their fiery hair until they die;
Then in the tower afar the watcher sees
The sun, that burned, less noble than it was,
Less noble still, until by dim degrees
No spark of him is specklike in his glass.
Then blind and dark in heaven the sun proceeds,
Vast, dead and hideous, knocking on his moons,
Till crashing on his like creation breeds,
Striking such life, a constellation swoons;
From dead things striking fire a new sun springs,
New fire, new life, new planets with new wings.

John Masefield

FAIRY THINGS

Grey lichens, mid thy hills of creeping thyme,
Grow like to fairy forests hung with rime;
And fairy money-pots are often found
That spring like little mushrooms out of ground,
Some shaped like cups and some in slender trim
Wineglasses like, that to the very rim
Are filled with little mystic shining seed;
We thought our fortunes promising indeed,
Expecting by and by ere night to find
Money ploughed up of more substantial kind.

Acres of little yellow seeds,
The wheat-field's constant blooms,
That ripen into prickly seeds
For fairy curry-combs,
To comb and clean the little things
That draw their nightly wain;
And so they scrub the beetle's wings
Till he can fly again.
And flannel felt for the beds of the queen
From the soft inside of the shell of the bean,
Where the gipsies down in the lonely dells
Had littered and left the plundered shells.

John Clare

DEWDROPS

The dewdrops on every blade of grass are so much like silver
drops that I am obliged to stoop down as I walk to see if they
are pearls, and those sprinkled on the ivy-woven beds of prim-
roses underneath the hazels, whitethorns, and maples are so
like gold beads that I stooped down to feel if they were hard,
but they melted from my finger. And where the dew lies on the
primrose, the violet and whitethorn leaves, they are emerald
and beryl, yet nothing more than the dews of the morning on
the budding leaves; nay, the road grasses are covered with gold
and silver beads, and the further we go the brighter they seem
to shine, like solid gold and silver. It is nothing more than the
sun's light and shade upon them in the dewy morning; every
thorn-point and every bramble-spear has its trembling orna-
ment: till the wind gets a little brisker, and then all is shaken
off, and all the shining jewelry passes away into a common
spring morning full of budding leaves, primroses, violets, vernal
speedwell, bluebell and orchids, and commonplace objects.

John Clare
Written in Northampton Asylum

PLEASANT SOUNDS

The rustling of leaves under the feet in woods and under hedges;
The crumping of cat-ice and snow down wood-rides, narrow
    lanes, and every street causeway;
Rustling through a wood or rather rushing, while the wind
    halloos in the oak-top like thunder;
The rustle of birds' wings startled from their nests or flying
    unseen into the bushes;
The whizzing of larger birds overhead in a wood, such as crows,
    puddocks, buzzards;
The trample of robins and woodlarks on the brown leaves, and
    the patter of squirrels on the green moss;
The fall of an acorn on the ground, the pattering of nuts on the
    hazel branches as they fall from ripeness;
The flirt of the groundlark's wing from the stubbles—how
    sweet such pictures on dewy mornings, when the dew
    flashes from its brown feathers!

John Clare
Written in Northampton Asylum

SHELLS

A curious child, who dwelt upon a tract
Of inland ground, applying to his ear
The convolutions of a smooth-lipped shell;
To which, in silence hushed, his very soul
Listened intensely; and his countenance soon
Brightened with joy; for murmurings from within
Were heard, sonorous cadences! whereby
To his belief, the monitor expressed
Mysterious union with his native sea.
Even in such a shell the Universe itself
Is to the ear of Faith: and there are times,
I doubt not, when to you it doth impart
Authentic tidings of invisible things;
Of ebb and flow and ever-during power;
And central peace, subsisting at the heart
Of endless agitation.

William Wordsworth

I have the shells now in a leather box—
Limpets and cowries, ones like hands spread out.
Lifeless they are yet bear the weight of doubt
And of desire with all its hidden shocks.

Once, as a child, I might have pressed the shell
Close to my ear and thought I heard the sea.
Now I hear absence sighing quietly.
I am the one who makes and pulls the bell.

You gathered these and so they bear your print.
I cannot see it, yet the simple knowing
That you have marked these shells keeps my love growing.
Passion can hide in any lifeless hint.

A sentiment perhaps, yet every gift
Carries the weight of all we did not do.
The shells are fragments and the fragments few,
But you still sound in what the shells have left.

Elizabeth Jennings

BLUEBELLS

Like smoke held down by frost
The bluebells wreathe in the wood,
Spring like a swan there
Feeds on a cold flood:

But the winter woodmen know
How to make flame
From sodden December faggots,
They can make the blue smoke climb.

Picked flowers wilt at once,
They flare but where they are;
The swan will not sing nor the fire thrive
In a town-watered jar:

But the winter woodmen know
The essential secret burning;
The fire at the earth's core
In touch with the turning sun.

Patric Dickinson

THE CROCUS

The winter night is round me like a skull,
Hollow and black, and time has rotted off;
The sky is void, the starry creeds are null,
And death is at the throat in a soft cough.

And rooted in the leaf-mould of the brain,
I see the crocus burn, sudden as spring,
Yet not of seasons, not of sun or rain,
Bright as a ghost in the skull's scaffolding.

It is not hope, this flower, nor love its light.
It makes the darkness glow, the silence chime;
Its life gives sense to death, names black with white—
The timeless flame that is the wick of time.

Norman Nicholson

MOONLIT APPLES

At the top of the house the apples are laid in rows,
And the skylight lets the moonlight in, and those
Apples are deep-sea apples of green. There goes
   A cloud on the moon in the autumn night.

A mouse in the wainscot scratches, and scratches, and then
There is no sound at the top of the house of men
Or mice; and the cloud is blown, and the moon again
   Dapples the apples with deep-sea light.

They are lying in rows there, under the gloomy beams;
On the sagging floor; they gather the silver streams
Out of the moon, those moonlit apples of dreams,
  And quiet is the steep stair under.

In the corridors under there is nothing but sleep.
And stiller than ever on orchard boughs they keep
Tryst with the moon, and deep is the silence, deep
  On moon-washed apples of wonder.

                                    John Drinkwater

THE GOD ON THE HEARTH

A god, a god sits on my hearth,
Laughs and plays with sober mirth,
Sings a small song, merry and wild,
As a bird might or a child.

Strayed here from some Olympian hill,
This god is rose and daffodil
Yet boils my kettle, cooks my dish,
Gives savour to the meats and fish.

I stretch my chilly hands above
And like my dog he fawns in love:
Licks at me with a playful tongue
And frisks, a bright thing, merry and young.

And yet so great a god is he,
You shall approach him on your knee,
Lest that his lightnings teach you awe,
This Burning Bush that Moses saw.

He is the Ark no hand may touch,
The Lily of Light without a smutch,
The Living Rose that none may take,
Caged in a gold and thorny brake.

This holy one stays with me still,
Singing his small song merry and shrill,
And hath so many things to do,
There is no time to grieve or rue.

For the great state he hath forgone,
The Lord Sun's dear companion,
Who toils and plays upon my hearth,
Nor yet forgets his starry birth.

Katharine Tynan

PART VI

CHILDREN AND LOVERS

A FLOWER GIVEN TO MY DAUGHTER

Frail the white rose and frail are
Her hands that gave
Whose soul is sere and paler
Than time's wan wave.

Rosefrail and fair—yet frailest
A wonder wild
In gentle eyes thou veilest,
My blueveined child.

James Joyce

A BABY ASLEEP AFTER PAIN

As a drenched, drowned bee
Hangs numb and heavy from a bending flower,
  So clings to me
My baby, her brown hair brushed with wet tears
  And laid against her cheek;
Her soft white legs hanging heavily over my arm
  Swing to my walking movement, weak
With after-pain. My sleeping baby hangs upon my life
  Like a burden she hangs on me;
She who had always seemed so light,
  Now wet with tears and pain hangs heavily,
  Even her floating hair sinks heavily
    Reaching downwards;
As the wings of a drenched, drowned bee
  Are a heaviness, and a weariness.

D. H. Lawrence

THE DANCE

She is young. Have I the right
Even to name her? Child,
It is no love I offer
Your quick limbs, your eyes;
Only the barren homage
Of an old man whom time
Crucifies. Take my hand
A moment in the dance,
Ignoring its sly pressure,
The dry rut of age,
And lead me under the boughs
Of innocence. Let me smell
My youth again in your hair.

R. S. Thomas

TO MISTRESS MARGERY WENTWORTH

With margeran[1] gentle,
  The flower of goodlihood,
Embroidered the mantle
  Is of your maidenhood.

Plainly I cannot glose[2]
  Ye be, as I divine
The pretty primèrose
  The goodly columbine.

With margeran gentle,
  The flower of goodlihood,
Embroidered the mantle
  Is of your maidenhood.

[1] marjoram.
[2] flatter.

Benign, courteous, and meek,
    With wordes well devised,
In you, who list to seek,
    Be virtues well comprised.

With margeran gentle,
    The flower of goodlihood,
Embroidered the mantle
    Is of your maidenhood.

John Skelton

LAURA

Rose-cheeked Laura, come;
Sing thou smoothly with thy beauty's
Silent music, either other
    Sweetly gracing.

Lovely forms do flow
From convent divinely framed;
Heaven is music, and thy beauty's
    Birth is heavenly.

These dull notes we sing
Discords need for helps to grace them;
Only beauty purely loving
    Knows no discord;

But still moves delight,
Like clear springs renewed by flowing,
Ever perfect, ever in them-
    selves eternal.

Thomas Campion

ECHOES

There was a boy; ye knew him well, ye cliffs
And islands of Winander!—many a time,
At evening, when the earliest stars began
To move along the edges of the hills,
Rising or setting, would he stand alone,
Beneath the trees, or by the glimmering lake;
And there, with fingers interwoven, both hands
Pressed closely palm to palm and to his mouth
Uplifted he, as through an instrument,
Blew mimic hootings to the silent owls,
That they might answer him. And then they would shout
Across the watery vale, and about again,
Responsive to his call, with quivering peals,
And long halloos, and screams, and echoes loud
Redoubled and redoubled; concourse wild
Of jocund din! And when a lengthened pause
Of silence came and baffled his best skill,
Then, sometimes, in that silence, while he hung
Listening, a gentle shock of mild surprise
Has carried far into his heart the voice
Of mountain torrents; or the visible scene
Would enter unawares into his mind
With all its solemn imagery, its rocks,
Its woods, and that uncertain heaven, received
Into the bosom of the steady lake.

William Wordsworth

BEDTIME STORY FOR MY SON

Where did the voice come from? I hunted through the rooms
For that small boy, that high, that head-voice,
The clatter as his heels caught on the door,
A shadow just caught moving through the door
Something like a school-satchel. My wife
Didn't seem afraid, even when it called for food
She smiled and turned her book and said:
'I couldn't go and love the empty air.'

We went to bed. Our dreams seemed full
Of boys in one or another guise, the paper-boy
Skidding along in grubby jeans, a music-lesson
She went out in the early afternoon to fetch a child from.
I pulled up from a pillow damp with heat
And saw her kissing hers, her legs were folded
Far away from mine. A pillow! It seemed
She couldn't love the empty air.

Perhaps, we thought, a child had come to grief
In some room in the old house we kept,
And listened if the noises came from some special room,
And then we'd take the boards up and discover
A pile of dusty bones like charcoal twigs and give
The tiny-sounding ghost a proper resting-place
So that it need not wander in the empty air.

No blood-stained attic harboured the floating sounds,
We found they came in rooms that we'd warmed with our life.
We traced the voice and found where it mostly came
From just underneath both our skins, and not only
In the night-time either, but at the height of noon
And when we sat at meals alone. Plainly, this is how we found
That loves pines loudly to go out to where
It need not spend itself on fancy and the empty air.

Peter Redgrove

THE MEETING

As I went up and he came down, my little six-year boy,
Upon the stairs we met and kissed, I and my tender Joy.
O fond and true, as lovers do, we kissed and clasped and parted;
And I went up and he went down, refreshed and happy-hearted.

What need was there for any words, his face against my face?
And in the silence heart to heart spoke for a little space

125

Of tender things and thoughts on wings and secrets none
  discovers;
And I went up and he went down, a pair of happy lovers.

His clinging arms about my neck, what need was there for
  words?
O little heart that beat so fast like any fluttering bird's!
'I love,' his silence said, 'I love,' my silence answered duly;
And I went up and he went down comforted wonderfully.

Katharine Tynan

A GARLAND OF PEACOCK FEATHERS

At daybreak, dawn of desire,
I trysted with my sweetheart,
Both bent on love, true passion,
In woodland aisle weaving song.
I asked my love, old as I,
To twine twigs from the saplings,
Pretty horns, a gay chaplet,
A garland for me, bright green.
'Fashion love's faultless circle,'
And the girl answered her bard:

'Pure your voice, skilful singing,
Know you not, complaint of pain,
It's a poor thing, no pleasure,
To strip birches till they die.
The birches have, gentle trees,
No leaves fit for the taking.
I'll not weave twigs together,
It's wrong to rob groves of leaves.'

She gave me, long it will last,
The gift I'll guard for ever,
Fine as gold cloth, a garland
Of peacock plumes for my head,
Superb chaplet, bright linen,

Pretty blossoms of gay plumes,
Lovely web of gleaming twigs,
Butterflies, leafy jewels.
Kingly work, it was comely,
Thickly piled, three-coloured wheels.
Dead men's eyes, glow-worm lanterns,
They are images of moons.
Good to have, never failing,
The mirrors from Virgil's fairs.

Long am I blessed, she gave it,
Garland for her glad-voiced bard.
Praiseworthy deed, her plying
And plaiting feathers and wings.

Slim girl's love-gift for her bard,
God gave it, pretty stripling,
All His care, craft of fine gold,
Bright as a gold pavilion.

Dafydd ap Gwilym

TRUE LOVE

My true love hath my heart and I have his,
  By just exchange one for another given;
I hold his dear, and mine he cannot miss,
  There never was a better bargain driven.
    My true love hath my heart and I have his.

His heart in me keeps him and me in one,
  My heart in him his thoughts and senses guides;
He loves my heart, for once it was his own,
  I cherish his, because in me it bides.
    My true love hath my heart and I have his.

Sir Philip Sidney

Let me not to the marriage of true minds
    Admit impediments. Love is not love
Which alters when it alteration finds,
    Or bends with the remover to remove.
O, no! it is an ever-fixéd mark,
    That looks on tempests and is never shaken;
It is the star to every wandering bark,
    Whose worth's unknown, although his height be taken.
Love's not Time's fool, though rosy lips and cheeks
    Within his bending sickle's compass come;
Love alters not with his brief hours and weeks,
    But bears it out even to the edge of doom,
      If this be error, and upon me proved,
      I never writ, nor no man ever loved.

William Shakespeare

'Come down, O maid, from yonder mountain height:
What pleasure lives in height (the shepherd sang)
In height and cold, the splendour of the hills?
But cease to move so near the Heavens, and cease
To glide a sunbeam by the blasted Pine,
To sit a star upon the sparkling spire;
And come, for Love is of the valley, come,
For Love is of the valley, come thou down
And find him; by the happy threshold, he,
Or hand in hand with Plenty in the maize,
Or red with spirted purple of the vats,
Or fox like in the vine; nor cares to walk
With Death and Morning on the silver horns,
Nor wilt thou snare him in the white ravine,
Nor find him dropt upon the firths of ice,
That huddling slant in furrow-cloven falls
To roll the torrent out of dusky doors:
But follow; let the torrent dance thee down
To find him in the valley; let the wild
Lean-headed Eagles yelp alone, and leave
The monstrous ledges there to slope, and spill
Their thousand wreaths of dangling water-smoke

That like a broken purpose waste in air:
So waste not thou; but come; for all the vales
Await thee; azure pillars of the hearth
Arise to thee; the children call, and I
Thy shepherd pipe, and sweet is every sound,
Sweeter thy voice, but every sound is sweet;
Myriads of rivulets hurrying thro' the lawn,
The moan of doves in immemorial elms,
And murmuring of innumerable bees.'

Lord Tennyson   from The Princess

A CITY FLOWER

To and fro from the City I go,
Tired of the ceaseless ebb and flow,
　　Sick of the crowded mart;
Tired of the din and rattle of wheels,
Sick of the dust as one who feels
　　The dust is over his heart.

And again and again, as the sunlight wanes,
I think of the lights in the leafy lanes,
　　With the bits of blue between;
And when about Rimmel's the perfumes play,
I smell no vapours of 'Ess Bouquet',
　　But violets hid in the green;
And I love—how I love—the plants that fill
The pots on my dust-dry window-sill,—
　　A sensitive sickly crop,—
But a flower that charms me more, I think,
Than cowslip, or crocus, or rose, or pink,
　　Blooms—in a milliner's shop.

Hazel eyes that wickedly peep
Flash, abash, and suddenly sleep
　　Under the lids drawn in;
Ripple of hair that rioteth out,
Mouth with a half-born smile and a pout,

And a baby breadth of chin;
Hands that light as the lighting bird,
On the bloom-bent bough, and the bough is stirred
    With a delicate ecstasy;
Fingers tipped with a roseate flush,
Flicking and flirting a feathery brush
    Over the papery bonnetry;—
Till the gauzy rose begins to glow,
And the gauzy hyacinths break and blow,
    And the dusty grape grows red;
And the flaunting grasses seem to say,
'Do we look like ornaments—tell us, we pray—
    Fit for a lady's head?'
And the butterfly wakes to a wiry life,
Like an elderly gentleman taking a wife,
    Knowing he must be gay,
And all the bonnets nid-noddle about,
Like chattering chaperons set at a rout,
    Quarrelling over their play.

How can I otherwise choose than look
At the beautiful face like a beautiful book,
    And learn a tiny part?
So I feel somehow that every day
Some flake of the dust is brushed away
    That had settled over my heart.

                                    Austin Dobson

URCEUS EXIT

    I intended an Ode,
        And it turned to a Sonnet.
    It began *à la mode*,
    I intended an Ode;
    But Rose crossed the road
        In her latest bonnet;
    I intended an Ode;
        And it turned to a Sonnet.

                                    Austin Dobson

THE BURIED LIFE

Light flows our war of mocking words, and yet,
Behold, with tears mine eyes are wet!
I feel a nameless sadness o'er me roll.
Yes, yes, we know that we can jest,
We know, we know that we can smile!
But there's something in this breast,
To which thy light words bring no rest.
And thy gay smiles no anodyne.
Give me thy hand, and hush awhile,
And turn those limpid eyes on mine,
And let me read there, love! thy inmost soul.

Alas! is even love too weak
To unlock the heart, and let it speak?
Are even lovers powerless to reveal
To one another what indeed they feel?
I knew the mass of men conceal'd
Their thoughts, for fear that if reveal'd
They would by other men be met
With blank indifference, or with blame reproved;
I knew they lived and moved
Trick'd in disguises, alien to the rest
Of men, and alien to themselves—and yet
The same heart beats in every human breast!

But we, my love!—does a like spell benumb
Our hearts, our voices?—must we too be dumb?

Ah, well for us, if even we,
Even for a moment, can get free
Our heart, and have our lips unchain'd;
For that which seals them hath been deep-ordain'd!

Fate, which foresaw
How frivolous a baby man would be—
By what distractions he would be possess'd,
How he would pour himself in every strife,
And well-nigh change his own identity—
That it might keep from his capricious play
His genuine self, and force him to obey

Even in his own despite his being's law,
Bade through the deep recesses of our breast
The unregarded river of our life
Pursue with indiscernible flow its way;
And that we should not see
The buried stream, and seem to be
Eddying at large in blind uncertainty,
Though driving on with it eternally.

But often, in the world's most crowded streets,
But often, in the din of strife,
There rises an unspeakable desire
After the knowledge of our buried life;
A thirst to spend our fire and restless force
In tracking out our true, original course;
A longing to inquire
Into the mystery of this heart which beats
So wild, so deep in us—to know
Whence our lives come and where they go.
And many a man in his own breast then delves,
But deep enough, alas! none ever mines.
And we have been on many thousand lines,
And we have shown, on each, spirit and power;
But hardly have we, for one little hour,
Been on our own line, have we been ourselves—
Hardly had skill to utter one of all
The nameless feelings that course through our breast,
But they course on for ever unexpress'd.
And long we try in vain to speak and act
Our hidden self, and what we say or do
Is eloquent, is well—but 'tis not true!
And then we will no more be rack'd
With inward striving, and demand
Of all the thousand nothings of the hour
Their stupefying power;
Ah yes, and they benumb us at our call!
Yet still, from time to time, vague and forlorn,
From the soul's subterranean depth upborne
As from an infinitely distant land,
Come airs, and floating echoes, and convey
A melancholy into all our day.

Only—but this is rare—
When a beloved hand is laid in ours.
When, jaded with the rush and glare
Of the interminable hours,
Our eyes can in another's eyes read clear,
When our world-deafen'd ear
Is by the tones of a loved voice caress'd—
A bolt is shot back somewhere in our breast,
And a lost pulse of feeling stirs again.
The eye sinks inward, and the heart lies plain,
And what we mean, we say, and what we would, we know,
A man becomes aware of his life's flow,
And hears its winding murmur; and he sees
The meadows where it glides, the sun, the breeze.
And there arrives a lull in the hot race
Wherein he doth for ever chase
That flying and elusive shadow, rest.
An air of coolness plays upon his face,
And an unwonted calm pervades his breast
And then he thinks he knows
The hills where his life rose,
And the sea where it goes.

Matthew Arnold

LONGING

Come to me in my dreams, and then
By day I shall be well again!
For then the night will more than pay
The hopeless longing of the day.

Come, as thou cam'st a thousand times,
A messenger from radiant climes,
And smile on thy new world, and be
As kind to others as to me!

Or, as thou never cam'st in sooth,
Come now, and let me dream it truth
And part my hair, and kiss my brow,
And say: *My love! why sufferest thou?*

Come to me in my dreams, and then
By day I shall be well again!
For then the night will more than pay
The hopeless longing of the day.

Matthew Arnold

HE WISHES FOR THE CLOTHS OF HEAVEN

Had I the heavens' embroidered cloths,
Enwrought with golden and silver light,
The blue and the dim and the dark cloths
Of night and light and the half-light,
I would spread the cloths under your feet:
But I, being poor, have only my dreams;
I have spread my dreams under your feet;
Tread softly because you tread on my dreams.

W. B. Yeats

THE FOLLY OF BEING COMFORTED

One that is ever kind said yesterday:
'Your well-beloved's hair has threads of grey,
And little shadows come about her eyes;
Time can but make it easier to be wise
Though now it seems impossible, and so
All that you need is patience.'

                        Heart cries, 'No,
I have not a crumb of comfort, not a grain.
Time can but make her beauty over again:
Because of that great nobleness of hers

The fire that stirs about her, when she stirs,
Burns but more clearly. O she had not these ways
When all the wild summer was in her gaze.'

O heart! O heart! if she'd but turn her head,
You'd know the folly of being comforted.

W. B. Yeats

ABSENCE

When my love was away,
Full three days were not sped,
I caught my fancy astray
    Thinking if she were dead.

And I alone, alone:
It seem'd in my misery
In all the world was none
Ever so lone as I.

I wept; but it did not shame
Nor comfort my heart: away
I rode as I might, and came
To my love at close of day.

The sight of her still'd my fears,
My fairest-hearted love:
And yet in her eyes were tears:
Which when I questioned of,

'O now thou art come,' she cried.
' 'Tis fled: but I thought to-day
I never could here abide,
If thou wert longer away.'

Robert Bridges

JUNE TWILIGHT

The twilight comes; the sun
  Dips down and sets,
The boys have done
  Play at the nets.

In a warm golden glow
  The woods are steeped.
The shadows grow;
  The bat has cheeped.

Sweet smells the new-mown hay;
  The mowers pass
Home, each his way,
  Through the grass.

The night-wind stirs the fern,
  A night-jar spins;
The windows burn
  In the inns.

Dusky it grows. The moon!
  The dews descend.
Love, can this beauty in our hearts
  end?

John Masefield

THE VISITING SEA

As the inhastening tide doth roll,
Home from the deep, along the whole
  Wide shining strand, and floods the caves,
  —Your love comes filling with happy waves
The open sea-shore of my soul.

But inland from the seaward spaces,
None knows, not even you, the places

Brimmed, at your coming, out of sight,
—The little solitudes of delight
This tide constrains in dim embraces.

You see the happy shore, wave-rimmed,
But know not of the quiet dimmed
    Rivers your coming floods and fills,
    The little pools 'mid happier hills,
My silent rivulets, over-brimmed.

What! I have secrets from you? Yes.
But, visiting Sea, your love doth press
    And reach in further than you know,
    And fills all these; and, when you go,
There's loneliness in loneliness.

Alice Meynell

AT NIGHT

To W.M.

Home, home from the horizon far and clear,
    Hither the soft wings sweep;
Flocks of the memories of the day draw near
    The dovecote doors of sleep.

Oh, which are they that come through sweetest light
    Of all these homing birds?
Which with the straightest and the swiftest flight?
    Your words to me, your words!

Alice Meynell

THE HOUSE OF LIFE

The life of the body's a cage,
    And the soul within it
Frets to escape, to be free,
    Like a lark or a linnet.

But since the struggle's in vain,
    She is weary ere long;
She chirps and she sings a little
    To assuage her wrong.

Behind the bars she sits brooding
    Her evil mishap,
Like a wild little hare or a rabbit
    That's caught in a trap,
Till, dazed with despair, she is weary,
    And struggles no more,
But plays with the sun and leaf-shadow
    That dance on the floor.

They call—they call to each other:
    O sister so small,
Are you there? Are you there, little brother,
    Behind the blank wall?
Like a bird, or a hare, or a rabbit,
    Frightened, undone,
The soul calls to another,
    That she be not alone.

Katharine Tynan

SONG

Why should your face so please me
That if one little line should stray
Bewilderment would seize me
And drag me down the tortuous way
Out of the moon into the night?
But so, into this tranquil light
You raise me.

How could our minds so marry
That, separate, blunder to and fro,
Make for a point, miscarry,

And blind as headstrong horses go?
Though now they in their promised land
At pleasure travel hand in hand
Or tarry.

This concord is an answer
To questions far beyond our mind
Whose image is a dancer.
All effort is to ease refined
Here, weight is light; this is the dove
Of love and peace, not heartless love
The lancer.

And yet I still must wonder
That such an armistice can be
And life roll by in thunder
To leave this calm with you and me.
This tranquil voice of silence, yes,
This single song of two, this is
A wonder.

Edwin Muir

Y IS FOR YOUTH

Would I had met you in my days of strength,
    Before my tide of life had turned, my Love;
These lightning streaks, that come in fitful starts,
    Are not the great forked lightnings you deserve;
Too many silver moons has my life worn
In an old thin rim, since I was born.

What you deserve are those enchanted notes
    We sing in dreams at night; so pure and sweet
That kings and queens sit down with bended heads,
    And listen with their crowns laid at their feet:
Those songs that pass, without a voice on Earth,
And perish in the brain that gives them birth.

W. H. Davies

THE VISITATION

Drowsing in my chair of disbelief
I watch the door as it slowly opens—
A trick of the night wind?

Your slender body seems a shaft of moonlight
Against the door as it gently closes.
Do you cast no shadow?

Your whisper is too soft for credence,
Your tread like blossom drifting from a bough,
Your touch even softer.

You wear that sorrowful and tender mask
Which on high mountain tops in heather-flow
Entrances lonely shepherds;

And though a single word scatters all doubts
I quake for wonder at your choice of me:
Why, why and why?

Robert Graves

MID-WINTER WAKING

Stirring suddenly from long hibernation,
I knew myself once more a poet
Guarded by timeless principalities
Against the worm of death, this hillside haunting;
And presently dared open both my eyes.

O gracious, lofty, shone against from under,
Back-of-the-mind-far clouds like towers;
And you, sudden warm airs that blow
Before the expected season of new blossom,
While sheep still gnaw at roots and lambless go—

Be witness that on waking, this mid-winter
I found her hand in mine laid closely
Who shall watch out the Spring with me.
We stared in silence all around us
But found no winter anywhere to see.

Robert Graves

THE THOUGHT

I will not write a poem for you,
because a poem, even the loveliest,
can only do what words can do—
stir the air, and dwindle, and be at rest.

Nor will I hold you with my hands, because
the bones of my hands on yours would press,
and you'd say after; 'Mortal was,
and crumbling, that lover's tenderness.'

But I will hold you in a thought without moving
spirit or desire or will—
for I know no other way of loving,
that endures when the heart is still.

Humbert Wolfe

HARBOUR

Your quiet and eager eyes wander about,
But, every now and then, return to me,
Contentedly, happily;
And I receive and fold them into mine.
Then my wild heart, though I may look so cool,
Breaks in a shout,
And calls along my body to my brain.
I (O, poor happy fool!)
—I suffer till I find your eyes again:
I want to make your strange eyes always mine.

Now, all your life stay with me! May that look
By which you seek me be my only book.
Your mind is like calm water. I have heard
Words like you, speak in the songs (of some wild bird).
Shall I grow tired of you? I want to die
Before we have to say Good-bye.

Messenger of love, shall we sit here
For ever? And when Time with angry hand
Raps for departure, let us both appear
Lost in our world of love;
We will not move:
We will pretend we do not understand.

No words are needful in the talk we have:
There is more faith in silence than in speech.
But all the little answers I can save
Lie in my heart, and, some time in the night,
They will arise and find their passage right;
And to the middle of your heart will send
Flying arrows of contented love:
We will lie there together, and not move.

Harold Monro

SONG

I sowed my wild oats
Before I was twenty.
Drunkards and turncoats
I knew in plenty.
Most friends betrayed me.
Each new affair
Further delayed me.
I didn't care.

I put no end to
The life that led me
The friends to lend to.

The bards who bled me.
Every bad penny
Finds its own robber.
My beds were many
And my cheques rubber.

Then, with the weather worse,
To the cold river,
I came reciting verse
With a hangover.
You shook a clammy hand.
How could I tell you
Then that wild oats died and
Brighter grain grew?

Now, once more wintertime,
We sit together.
In your bright forelock Time
Gives me fair weather.
Soon will a summer break
Well worth the having.
Then shall our hearts awake
Into our loving.

Dom Moraes

THE FINAL WORD

Since I was ten I have not been unkind
To anyone save those who were most close:
Of my close friends one of the best is blind,
One deaf, and one a priest who can't write prose.
None has a quiet mind.

Deep into night my friends with tired faces
Break language up for one word to remain,
The tall forgiving word nothing effaces,
Though without maps it travel, and explain
A pure truth in all places.

Yet death, if it should fall on us, would be
Only the smallest settling into beds:
Our last word lost because Eternity
Made its loud noise above our lifted heads
Before we ceased to see.

But, all made blind and deaf, the final word
Bequeathed by us, at the far side of
Experience, waits: there neither man nor bird
Settles, except with knowledge, or much love.
There Adam's voice is heard.

And my true love, a skylark in each eye,
Walks the small grass, and the small frightened things
Scurry to her for comfort, and can't die
While she still lives, and all the broken Kings
Kneel to her and know why.

Because she turns, her love at last expressed,
Into my arms: and then I cannot die.
I have furnished my heart to be her nest
For even if at dusk she chooses to fly
Afterwards she must rest.

Dom Moraes

THE VISITORS

They visit me and I attempt to keep
A social smile upon my face. Even here
Some ceremony is required, no deep
Relationship, simply a way to clear
    Emotion to one side; the fear
I felt last night is buried in drugged sleep.

They come and all their kindness makes me want
To cry (they say the sick weep easily).
When they have gone I shall be limp and faint,

My heart will thump and stumble crazily;
 Yet through my illness I can see
One wish stand clear no pain, no fear can taint.

Your absence has been stronger than all pain
And I am glad to find that when most weak
Always my mind returned to you again.
Through all the noisy nights when, harsh awake,
 I longed for day and light to break—
In that sick desert, you were life, were rain.

         Elizabeth Jennings

LOVE'S MATRIMONY

There is no happy life
But in a wife;
The comforts are so sweet
When they do meet:
'Tis plenty, peace, a calm
Like dropping balm:
Love's weather is so fair,
Perfumed air,
Each word such pleasure brings
Like soft-touched strings:
Love's passion moves the heart
On either part.
Such harmony together,
So pleased in either,
No discords, concords still,
Sealed with one will.
By love, God man made one,
Yet not alone:
Like stamps of king and queen
It may be seen,
Two figures but one coin;
So they do join,
Only they not embrace,
We, face to face.

    William Cavendish, Duke of Newcastle

TO MY WIFE

I know you, wife;
Know you as life crumples your clothes,
Weaves at your face, and passes.
In some part of the milkman's world
You are a smile. Shopkeepers and friends
Gleam in its separate lights and think
They understand. All that our children know
Of you warms them like their blankets,
Tucked by your everlasting hands.
But I, for whom these things
Mean new expenses and the loss of you,
Know you as a bird can know its wings,
A salmon its return.
You have left sounds in every room
Protecting me from loneliness, and if
One day I take a car
And find a land to plunder where your face
Does not arrest me like a fundamental law,
Necessity will teach me
That your name is Love.

Peter Firth

Part VII

LOVE'S LAMENTS

TEARS

Weep you no more, sad fountains;
  What need you flow so fast?
Look how the snowy mountains
  Heaven's sun doth gently waste!
But my Sun's heavenly eyes
    View not your weeping,
    That now lies sleeping
Softly, now softly lies
    Sleeping.

Sleep is a reconciling,
  A rest that peace begets;
Doth not the sun rise smiling
  When fair at even he sets?
Rest you then, rest, sad eyes!
    Melt not in weeping
    While she lies sleeping
Softly, now softly lies
    Sleeping.

John Dowland

Follow thy fair sun, unhappy shadow.
  Though thou be black as night,
  And she made all of light,
Yet follow thy fair sun, unhappy shadow.

Follow her whose light thy light depriveth.
  Though here thou livest disgraced,
  And she in heaven is placed,
Yet follow her whose light the world reviveth.

Follow those pure beams whose beauty burneth,
    That so have scorched thee,
    As thou still black must be,
Till her kind beams thy black to brightness turneth.

Follow her, while yet her glory shineth.
    There comes a luckless night,
    That will dim all her light;
And this the black unhappy shade divineth.

Follow still, since so thy fates ordained.
    The sun must have his shade,
    Till both at once do fade,
The sun still proved, the shadow still disdained.

Thomas Campion

REQUIESCAT

Strew on her roses, roses,
    And never a spray of yew!
In quiet she reposes;
    Ah, would that I did too!

Her mirth the world required;
    She bathed it in smiles of glee.
But her heart was tired, tired,
    And now they let her be.

Her life was turning, turning,
    In mazes of heat and sound.
But for peace her soul was yearning,
    And now peace laps her round.

Her cabin'd, ample spirit,
    It flutter'd and fail'd for breath.
To-night it doth inherit
    The vasty hall of death.

Matthew Arnold

DOVER BEACH

The sea is calm tonight.
The tide is full, the moon lies fair
Upon the straits;—on the French coast the light
Gleams and is gone; the cliffs of England stand,
Glimmering and vast, out in the tranquil bay.
Come to the window, sweet is the night-air!
Only, from the long line of spray
Where the sea meets the moon-blanch'd land,
Listen! you hear the grating roar
Of pebbles which the waves draw back, and fling,
At their return, up the high strand,
Begin, and cease, and then again begin,
With tremulous cadence slow, and bring
The eternal note of sadness in.

Sophocles long ago
Heard it on the Aegaean, and it brought
Into his mind the turbid ebb and flow
Of human misery; we
Find also in the sound a thought,
Hearing it by this distant northern sea.

The Sea of Faith
Was once, too, at the full, and round earth's shore
Lay like the folds of a bright girdle furl'd.
But now I only hear
Its melancholy, long, withdrawing roar,
Retreating, to the breath
Of the night-wind, down the vast edges drear
And naked shingles of the world.

Ah, love, let us be true
To one another! for the world, which seems
To lie before us like a land of dreams,
So various, so beautiful, so new,
Hath really neither joy, nor love, nor light,
Nor certitude, nor peace, nor help for pain;
And we are here as on a darkling plain
Swept with confused alarms of struggle and flight,
Where ignorant armies clash by night.

Matthew Arnold

When I have fears that I may cease to be
    Before my pen has glean'd my teaming brain,
Before high-piled books, in charact'ry,
    Hold like full garners the full-ripen'd grain;
When I behold, upon the night's starr'd face,
    Huge cloudy symbols of a high romance,
And feel that I may never live to trace
    Their shadows, with the magic hand of chance;
And when I feel, fair creature of an hour,
    That I shall never look upon thee more,
Never have relish in the faery bower
    Of unreflecting love!—then on the shore
Of the wide world I stand alone, and think,
Till Love and Fame to nothingness do sink.

                                        John Keats

REMEMBRANCE

Cold in the earth—and the deep snow piled above thee,
Far, far removed, cold in the dreary grave!
Have I forgot, my only Love, to love thee,
Severed at last by Time's all-severing wave?

Now, when alone, do my thoughts no longer hover
Over the mountains, on that northern shore,
Resting their wings where heath and fern-leaves cover
Thy noble heart for ever, ever more?

Cold in the earth—and fifteen wild Decembers
From those brown hills have melted into spring:
Faithful, indeed, is the spirit that remembers
After such years of change and suffering!

Sweet Love of youth, forgive, if I forget thee,
While the world's tide is bearing me along;
Other desires and other hopes beset me,
Hopes which obscure, but cannot do thee wrong!

No later light has lightened up my heaven,
No second morn[1] has ever shone for me;
All my life's bliss from thy dear life was given,
All my life's bliss is in the grave with thee.

But, when the days of golden dreams had perished,
And even Despair was powerless to destroy,
Then did I learn how existence could be cherished,
Strengthened, and fed, without the aid of joy.

Then did I check the tears of useless passion—
Weaned my young soul from yearning after thine;
Sternly denied its burning wish to hasten
Down to that tomb already more than mine.

And, even yet, I dare not let it languish,
Dare not indulge in memory's rapturous pain;
Once drinking deep of that divinest anguish,
How could I seek the empty world again?

Emily Brontë

THE APPEAL

If grief for grief can touch thee,
    If answering woe for woe,
If any ruth can melt thee,
    Come to me now!

I cannot be more lonely,
    More drear I cannot be!
My worn heart throbs so wildly,
    'Twill break for thee.

And when the world despises,
    When Heaven repels my prayer,
Will not mine angel comfort?
    Mine idol hear?

[1] 'moon' in one ms.

Yes, by the tears I've poured thee,
    By all my hours of pain,
Oh, I shall surely win thee,
    Beloved, again!

Emily Brontë

THE LOVE SONG OF HAR DYAL

Alone upon the housetops to the North
I turn and watch the lightning in the sky—
The glamour of thy footsteps in the North.
Come back to me, Beloved, or I die.

Below my feet the still bazaar is laid—
Far, far below the weary camels lie—
The camels and the captives of thy raid.
Come back to me, Beloved, or I die!

My father's wife is old and harsh with years
And drudge of all my father's house am I—
My bread is sorrow and my drink is tears.
Come back to me, Beloved, or I die!

Rudyard Kipling

SONNET ON THE DEATH OF HIS WIFE
(*From the Portuguese of Antonio di Ferreiro*)

That blessed sunlight, that once showed to me
My way to heaven more plain, more certainly,
And with her bright beams banished utterly
All trace of mortal sorrow far from me,
Has gone from me, has left her prison sad,
And I am blind and alone and gone astray,
Like a lost pilgrim on a desert way
Wanting the blessed guide that once he had.

Thus with a spirit bowed and mind a blur
I trace the holy steps where she has gone
By valleys and by meadows and by mountains,
And everywhere I catch a glimpse of her,
She takes me by the hand and leads me on,
And my eyes follow her—my eyes made fountains.

John Masefield

WHEN YOU ARE OLD

When you are old and grey and full of sleep,
And nodding by the fire, take down this book,
And slowly read, and dream of the soft look
Your eyes had once, and of their shadows deep;

How many loved your moments of glad grace,
And loved your beauty with love false or true,
But one man loved the pilgrim soul in you,
And loved the sorrows of your changing face;

And bending down beside the glowing bars,
Murmur, a little sadly, how Love fled
And paced upon the mountains overhead
And hid his face amid a crowd of stars.

W. B. Yeats

SONG

O lady, when the tipped cup of the moon blessed you
You became soft fire with a cloud's grace;
The difficult stars swam for eyes in your face;
You stood, and your shadow was my place:
You turned, your shadow turned to ice,
    O my lady.

O lady, when the sea caressed you
You were a marble of foam, but dumb.
When will the stone open its tomb?
When will the waves give over their foam?
You will not die, nor come home,
    O my lady.

O lady, when the wind kissed you
You made him music for you were a shaped shell.
I follow the waters and the wind still
Since my heart heard it and all to pieces fell
Which your lovers stole, meaning ill,
    O my lady.

O lady, consider when I shall have lost you
The moon's full hands, scattering waste,
The sea's hands, dark from the world's breast,
The world's decay where the wind's hands have passed,
And my head, worn out with love, at rest
In my hands, and my hands full of dust,
    O my lady.

Ted Hughes

PART VIII

VISIONS AND DREAMS OF PEACE

CHORUS FROM HIPPOLYTUS

Could I take me to some cavern for mine hiding,
   In the hill-tops where the Sun scarce hath trod;
Or a cloud make the home of my abiding,
   As a bird among the bird-droves of God!
     Could I wing me to my rest amid the roar
     Of the deep Adriatic on the shore,
Where the water of Eridanus is clear,
   And Phaëthon's sad sisters by his grave
Weep into the river, and each tear
   Gleams, a drop of amber, in the wave!

To the strand of the Daughters of the Sunset,
   The Apple-tree, the singing and the gold;
Where the mariner must stay him from his onset,
   And the red wave is tranquil as of old;
     Yea, beyond that Pillar of the End
     That Atlas guardeth, would I wend;
Where a voice of living water never ceaseth
   In God's quiet garden by the sea,
And Earth, the ancient life-giver, increaseth
   Joy among the meadows, like a tree.

              Euripides   Translated by Gilbert Murray

For once in a dream or trance I saw the gods
Each sitting on the top of his mountain-isle,
While down below the little ships sailed by,
Toy multitudes swarmed in the harbours, shepherds drove
Their tiny flocks to the pastures, marriage feasts
Went on below, small birthdays and holidays,
Ploughing and harvesting and life and death,
And all permissible, all acceptable,
Clear and secure as in a limpid dream.

But they, the gods, as large and bright as clouds,
Conversed across the sounds in tranquil voices
High in the sky above the untroubled sea,
And their eternal dialogue was peace
Where all these things were woven, and this our life
Was as a chord deep in that dialogue,
As easy utterance of harmonious words,
Spontaneous syllables bodying forth a world.

Edwin Muir

THE OLD SHIPS

I have seen old ships sail like swans asleep
Beyond the village which men still call Tyre,
With leaden age o'ercargoed, dipping deep
For Famagusta and the hidden sun
That rings black Cyprus with a lake of fire;
And all those ships were certainly so old
Who knows how oft with squat and noisy gun,
Questing brown slaves or Syrian oranges,
The pirate Genoese
Hell-raked them till they rolled
Blood, water, fruit and corpses up the hold.
But now through friendly seas they softly run,
Painted the mid-sea blue or shore-sea green,
Still patterned with the vine and grapes in gold.

But I have seen,
Pointing her shapely shadows from the dawn
An image tumbled on a rose-swept bay,
A drowsy ship of some yet older day;
And, wonder's breath indrawn,
Thought I—who knows—who knows—but in that same
(Fished up beyond Aeaea, patched up new
—Stern painted brighter blue—)
That talkative, bald-headed seaman came
(Twelve patient comrades sweating at the oar)
From Troy's doom-crimson shore,

And with great lies about his wooden horse
Set the crew laughing, and forgot his course.
It was so old a ship—who knows, who knows?
—And yet so beautiful, I watched in vain
To see the mast burst open with a rose,
And the whole deck put on its leaves again.

James Elroy Flecker

THE PEACE OF EDEN

Morning

. . . His mouth rounded fleetingly for the *h'wee-ee* whistle-call, formed *wé-e-na* in a sigh of breath as his hands spread the sky out; *h'wee-wéna*, the bird. . . .

A moment, and his eyes found it yellow on a pink-flowering spray: yellow and blue as the little wings spanned for flight, no more than the spread of his fingers. The spray dipped once and lifted, and was empty. More blue than yellow on the wing to his outstretched hand, the bird ringed his finger lightly to perch, little head cocked, a bright eye watchful: and through its beak a wisp of pale stem. He had not seen the stem until now.

—Has the Lord God given it to you? Adam said.

For meat, he supposed: and he watched, still, to see how it would eat such a thing.

—Eat, then. Go on.

But it hopped on his finger to face the stream, the stem held as before. He lifted his hand and it flew off, swooping low over the water, two birds, a bird above and a bird beneath, wing tips meeting an instant briefly at the surface then apart: the gazelle's head and the leopard's lifted up, and the blue gone in high among the little leaves; the little top-most leaves that stood on the air, shot through with sunshine, and the blue between was the sky blue. . . .

Mid-day

Adam, moving upstream at a trot, the river on his left hand, heard the leopard through a wall of rushes on his right: the crown of a sapling agitated violently above the reed-plumes. He broke through and came upon the leopard stripping the tender bark below with claw and fang, and tumbled it nose over tail in among the rushes laughing, Make way! Make way! before it had properly turned at his coming. It struck out once and he caught and pinned it, fingers gripped deep in the fur. And then, loosing his hold, he crumpled its two ears in his hands until it rolled over and purred: and tiring of this, left it and went on alone. . . .

Evening

Adam had come walking with the presence of the Lord God. . . .

In the dying light only the street of the thán was certain, the tháneve where it lay gleaming: the river beautiful, and the darker mass of the trees over beyond it. Under the nearer trees also the shadows gathered, sealing up the garden in a mystery, holding its depths secret as the river did, and strange.

Somewhere behind Adam as he stood a creature called plaintively, which he could not name, riff-riff-riff . . . and was quiet.

He shifted a little and stood on one leg, aware of the night air on his body, and it was as if it had been himself calling, out of some mood that was neither cold nor hunger, nor thirsting, and had no name. Lord . . . Even before he whispered it, without knowing why he whispered, turning in the darkness to the presence of the Lord God, the thought came to him that he was alone.

—Elohim . . . ?

—My son.

In the darkness Adam sighed, smiling, and rubbed the flesh of his arm. The stars came one by one to the surface of the river, and the pale moon floating. He moved his feet, glancing back towards the shelter of the forest; turned back a little way, and hesitated. Will you come with me?

—I am with you always.

He went on then in under the black branches, thrusting the boughs of them aside to pass through, stumbling among familiar things: ferncrunch underfoot and the dry bracken smell of it, smooth tree bole against his palms, and the rough kiss of the fronds. He smiled again at the startled hustlings his passage wakened close at hand, the companionship of small creatures scurrying and pattering out of his path. As his eyes grew accustomed to the want of light he went more surely, learning to distinguish shadow from shadow, and the deeper pools of the hollows before his foot trod into them. The furriness of catkins, brushing his arm, made him think of the leopard, and he stopped on the thought and drew a long breath to call it up, shattering the night. There was no answering call, and when he would have called again his jaw locked in a yawn. There was moonlight enough by now to show him he leaned on a bank tall with grass, in a grove. He yawned again, pressing his eyes, and surveyed it. There was a place under the bank itself where it was level, and he trod the grass down in a circle, kneeling to smooth it with his hands.

Before he was properly asleep the leopard came to him, coming through the night with no sound at all, he heard nothing. Lying on his back, he looked up and saw the amber eyes on the bank. A cloud passed across the moon, above the treetops, and he heard the leopard drop down. He felt the weight of it in the grass beside him. His outstretched hand told him of the comfortable purring through the warmth of fur, the claws that stretched out and withdrew softly, gently grazing his arm.

David Bolt

POEM FOR PSYCHOANALYSTS AND/OR THEOLOGIANS

> Naked apples, woolly-coated peaches
> Swelled on the garden's wall. Unbounded
> Odour of windless, spice-bearing trees
> Surrounded my lying in sacred turf,
> Made dense the guarded air—the forest of trees
> Buoyed up therein like weeds in ocean
> Lived without motion. I was the pearl,
> Mother-of-pearl my bower. Milk-white the cirrhus
> Streaked the blue egg-shell of the distant sky,
> Early and distant, over the spicy forest;

Wise was the fangless serpent, drowsy.
All this, indeed, I do not remember.
I remember the remembering, when first walking
I heard the golden gates behind me
Fall to, shut fast. On the flinty road,
Black-frosty, blown on with an eastern wind,
I found my feet. Forth on journey,
Gathering this garment over aching bones,
I went. I wander still. But the world is round.

C. S. Lewis

THE WILD TREES

O the wild trees of my home,
forests of blue dividing the pink moon,
the iron blue of those ancient branches
with their berries of vermilion stars.

In that place of steep meadows
the stacked sheaves are roasting,
and the sun-torn tulips
are tinders of scented ashes.

But here I have lost
the dialect of your hills,
my tongue has gone blind
far from their limestone roots.

Through trunks of black elder
runs a fox like a lantern,
and the hot grasses sing
with the slumber of larks.

But here there are thickets
of many different gestures,
torn branches of brick and steel
frozen against the sky.

O the wild trees of home
with their sounding dresses,
locks powdered with butterflies
and cheeks of blue moss.

I want to see you rise
from my brain's dry river,
I want your lips of wet roses
laid over my eyes.

O fountains of earth and rock,
gardens perfumed with cucumber,
home of secret valleys
where the wild trees grow.

Let me return at last
to your fertile wilderness,
to sleep with the coiled fernleaves
in your heart's live stone.

Laurie Lee

  So she was gently glad to see him laid
Under her favourite bower's quiet shade,
On her own couch, new made of flower leaves,
Dried carefully on the cooler side of sheaves
When last the sun his autumn tresses shook,
And the tann'd harvesters rich armfuls took.
Soon was he quieted to slumbrous rest:
But, ere it crept upon him, he had prest
Peona's busy hand against his lips,
And still, a-sleeping, held her finger-tips
In tender pressure. And as a willow keeps
A patient watch over the stream that creeps
Windingly by it, so the quiet maid
Held her in peace: so that a whispering blade
Of grass, a wailful gnat, a bee bustling
Down in the blue-bells, or a wren light rustling
Among sere leaves and twigs, might all be heard.

O magic sleep! O comfortable bird,
That broodest o'er the troubled sea of the mind
Till it is hush'd and smooth! O unconfined
Restraint! imprison'd liberty! great key
To golden palaces, strange minstrelsy,
Fountains grotesque, new trees, bespangled caves,
Echoing grottos, full of tumbling waves
And moonlight; aye, to all the mazy world
Of silvery enchantment!—who, unfurl'd
Beneath thy drowsy wing a triple hour,
But renovates and lives?—Thus, in the bower,
Endymion was calm'd to life again.

John Keats   from Endymion

Spirits walking everywhere,
Thrown up like fountains
Then sinking into the ground,
Walking among the trees
That seem fast
So slowly do they well up
And sink down.

But to me the landscape is like a sea
the waves of the hills
and the bubbles of bush and flower
and the springtide breaking into white foam!

It is a slow sea,
Mare tranquillum,
And a thousand years of wind
Cannot raise a dwarf billow to the moonlight.

But the bosom of the landscape lifts and falls
With its own leaden tide,
That tide whose sparkles are the lilliputian stars.

It is that slow sea
That sea of adamantine languor,
Sleep!

Walter James Turner   from The Seven Days of the Sun

LANDSCAPE, BY CH'ENG SUI

From a mountainside,
We look dizzily down
Through an ancient willow.

Across the bay
The peninsulas of rocks and trees
Fan the mist away
Into a poem on
A last inch of sky,
Indelible horizon.

In a narrow boat
Curved and shallow as a leaf,
A lady and her boatman float
Upon the mist that hangs
Under and over their watery way.

She sits, with her white
Face lighting her black hair,
In the pale robe of ceremony.

The boatman in a pointed hat
Poles with dark hands
Their fragile craft
Towards a distant shore,
Where, set in a dry cliff among
Dark pines, a little house invents

A figure watching from an upper window
A dry leaf drifting on the misty bay.

James Kirkup

STREET LAMPS

Gold, with an innermost speck
Of silver, singing afloat
 Beneath the night,
Like balls of thistledown
Wandering up and down
 Seeking where to alight!

Slowly, above the street,
Above the ebb of feet
 Drifting in flight;
Still, in the purple distance
The gold of their strange persistence
As they cross and part and meet
 And pass out of sight!

The seed-ball of the sun
Is broken at last, and done
 Is the orb of day.
Now to their separate ends
Seed after day-seed wends
 A separate way.

No sun will ever rise
Again on the wonted skies
 In the midst of the spheres.
The globe of the day, over-ripe,
Is shattered at last beneath the stripe
Of the wind, and its oneness veers
 Out myriad-wise.

Seed after seed after seed
Drifts over the town, in its need
 To sink and have done;
To settle at last in the dark,
To bury its weary spark
 Where the end is begun.

Darkness, and depth of sleep,
Nothing to know or to weep

Where the seed sinks in
To the earth of the under-night
Where all is silent, quite
Still, and the darknesses steep
    Out all the sin.

                D. H. Lawrence

NONENTITY

The stars that open and shut
Fall on my shallow breast
Like stars on a pool.

The soft wind, blowing cool,
Laps little crest after crest
Of ripples across my breast.

And dark grass under my feet
Seems to dabble in me
Like grass in a brook.

Oh, and it is sweet
To be all these things, not to be
Any more myself.

For look,
I am weary of myself.

                D. H. Lawrence

A DREAM

This is a strange twilit country, but full of peace.
Faintly I hear sorrow; she sighs, moving away.
She goes, and guilt goes with her; all is forgiven.
Grey wolds and a slow dark river spell release

In this place where it is never quite night or day,
More like the elysian fields than the fields of heaven;

And no one here but I and this silent child.
She needs to sleep, I will carry her through the dim
Levels of this long river's deliberate mazes.
Nothing of man's is here, and never a wild
Creature to crop the grass or tunnel the brim
Of the full stream, or look up in our two faces.

She spoke so strangely that once, but she speaks no more.
Leans her head down in my neck, and is light to bear.
I think she walked here over the twilit stream.
I must find the tree, the elm by the river-shore,
Loosen her little arms and leave her there,
Under the boughs of sleep and the leaves of dream.

Ruth Pitter

A PINCH OF SALT

(Dream Bird)

When a dream is born in you
  With a sudden clamorous pain,
When you know the dream is true
  And lovely, with no flaw or stain,
O then be careful, or with sudden clutch
You'll hurt the delicate thing you prize so much.

Dreams are like a bird that mocks,
  Flirting the feathers of his tail.
When you seize at the salt-box
  Over the hedge you'll see him sail.
Old birds are neither caught with salt or chaff:
They watch you from the apple bough and laugh.

Poet, never chase the dream.
  Laugh yourself and turn away.

Mask your hunger, let it seem
    Small matter is he come or stay;
And when he nestles in your hand at last,
Close up your fingers tight and hold him fast.

Robert Graves

THROUGH NIGHTMARE

Never be disenchanted of
That place you sometimes dream yourself into.
Lying at large remove beyond all dream,
Or those you find there, though but seldom
In their company seated—

The untameable, the live, the gentle,
Have you not known them? Whom? They carry
Time looped so river-wise about their house
There's no way in by history's road
To name or number them.

In your sleepy eyes I read the journey
Of which disjointedly you tell; which stirs
My loving admiration, that you should travel
Through nightmare to a lost and moated land,
Who are timorous by nature.

Robert Graves

RENOUNCEMENT

I must not think of thee; and, tired yet strong,
I shun the love that lurks in all delight—
    The love of thee—and in the blue heaven's height,
And in the dearest passage of a song.
Oh, just beyond the sweetest thoughts that throng
    This breast, the thought of thee waits hidden yet bright;

But it must never, never come in sight;
I must stop short of thee the whole day long.
  When night gives pause to the long watch I keep,
And all my bonds I needs must loose apart,
Must doff my will as raiment laid away—
But when sleep comes to close each difficult day,
  With the first dream that comes with the first sleep
I run, I run, I am gather'd to thy heart.

Alice Meynell

THE COURTS

A Figure of the Epiphany

The poet's imageries are noble ways,
Approaches to a plot, an open shrine.
Their splendours, colours, avenues, arrays,
    Their courts that run with wine;

Beautiful similies, 'fair and fragrant things,'
Enriched, enamouring,—raptures, metaphors
Enhancing life, are paths for pilgrim kings
    Made free of golden doors.

And yet the open heavenward plot, with dew,
Ultimate poetry, enclosed, enskied,
(Albeit such ceremonies lead thereto)
    Stands on the yonder side.

Plain, behind oracles, it is; and past
All symbols, simple; perfect, heavenly-wild,
The song some loaded poets reach at last—
    The kings that found a Child.

Alice Meynell

THE MAGI

Now as at all times I can see in the mind's eye,
In their stiff, painted clothes, the pale unsatisfied ones
Appear and disappear in the blue depths of the sky
With all their ancient faces like rain-beaten stones,
And all their helms of silver hovering side by side,
And all their eyes fixed, hoping to find once more,
Being of Calvary's turbulence unsatisfied,
The uncontrollable mystery on the bestial floor.

W. B. Yeats

SAILING TO BYZANTIUM

I

That is no country for old men. The young
In one another's arms, birds in the trees,
—Those dying generations—at their song,
The salmon-falls, the mackerel-crowded seas,
Fish, flesh, or fowl, commend all summer long
Whatever is begotten, born, and dies.
Caught in that sensual music all neglect
Monuments of unageing intellect.

II

An aged man is but a paltry thing,
A tattered coat upon a stick, unless
Soul claps its hands and sing, and louder sing
For every tatter in its mortal dress,
Nor is there singing school but studying
Monuments of its own magnificence;
And therefore I have sailed the seas and come
To the holy city of Byzantium.

III

O sages standing in God's holy fire
As in the gold mosaic of a wall,
Come from the holy fire, perne in a gyre,

And be the singing-master of my soul.
Consume my heart away; sick with desire
And fastened to a dying animal
It knows not what it is; and gather me
Into the sacrifice of eternity.

IV

Once out of nature I shall never take
My bodily form from any natural thing,
But such a form as Grecian goldsmiths make
Of hammered gold and gold enamelling
To keep a drowsy Emperor awake;
Or set upon a golden bough to sing
To lords and ladies of Byzantium
Of what is past, or passing, or to come.

W. B. Yeats

THE CLIMATE OF THOUGHT

The climate of thought has seldom been described.
It is no terror of Caucasian frost,
Nor yet that brooding Hindu heat
For which a loin-rag and a dish of rice
Suffice until the pestilent monsoon.
But, without winter, blood would run too thin;
Or, without summer, fires would burn too long.
In thought the seasons run concurrently.

Thought has a sea to gaze, not voyage, on
And hills, to rough the edge of the bland sky,
Not to be climbed in search of blander prospect;
Few birds, sufficient for such caterpillars
As are not fated to turn butterflies;
Few butterflies, sufficient for such flowers
As are the luxury of a full orchard;
Wind, sometimes, in the evening chimneys; rain
On the early morning roof, on sleepy sight;
Snow streaked upon the hilltop, feeding

The fond brook at the valley-head
That greens the valley and that parts the lips;
The sun, simple, like a country neighbour;
The moon, grand, not fanciful with clouds.

Robert Graves

ONCE

Once would the early sun steal in through my eastern window,
    A sea of time ago;
Tracing a stealthy trellis of shadow across the pictures
    With his gilding trembling glow;
Brimming my mind with rapture, as though of some alien spirit,
    In those eternal hours
I spent with my self as a child; alone, in a world of wonder—
    Air, and light and flowers;
Tenderness, longing, grief, intermingling with bodiless beings
    Shared else with none:
How would desire flame up in my soul; with what passionate
  yearning
    As the rays stole soundlessly on!—
Rays such as Rembrandt adored, such as dwell on the faces of
  seraphs,
    Wings-folded, solemn head,
Piercing the mortal with sorrow past all comprehension. . . .
    Little of that I read
In those shadowy runes in my bedroom. But one wild notion
    Made my heart with tears overflow—
The knowledge that love unsought, unspoken, unshared,
  unbetokened,
    Had mastered me through and through:
And yet—the children we are!—that naught of its ardour and
  beauty
    Even the loved should know.

Walter de la Mare

REAL PROPERTY

Tell me about that harvest field.
Oh! Fifty acres of living bread.
The colour has painted itself in my heart.
The form is patterned in my head.

So now I take it everywhere;
See it whenever I look round;
Hear it growing through every sound,
Know exactly the sound it makes—
Remembering, as one must all day,
Under the pavement the live earth aches.

Trees are at the farther end,
Limes all full of the mumbling bee:
So there must be a harvest field
Whenever one thinks of a linden tree.

A hedge is about it, very tall,
Hazy and cool, and breathing sweet.
Round paradise is such a wall
And all the day, in such a way,
In paradise the wild birds call.

You only need to close your eyes
And go within your secret mind,
And you'll be into paradise:
I've learnt quite easily to find
Some linden trees and drowsy bees,
A tall sweet hedge with the corn behind.

I will not have that harvest mown:
I'll keep the corn and leave the bread.
I've bought that field; it's now my own:
I've fifty acres in my head.
I take it as a dream to bed.
I carry it about all day. . . .

Sometimes when I have found a friend
I give a blade of corn away.

Harold Monro

A CHORISTER IN AVALON

When in the glass I see the heavy clay
  of which I am compact, I also see
a tall companion at my shoulder sway—
  the golden ghost a god designed for me.

He is all fire, as I am smouldering ash,
  he is all freedom, as I am straitly bound,
he is all spirit, I the sullen flesh,
  the body of Christ is He, and I the wound.

He does not rebuke, he does not pity me,
  for I am only the shadow he has cast
in another star, where earth is a memory
  of something small and dark that ends at last.

It is the true star, rising in the hush
  of a heaven that is wholly in the mind,
but passes out beyond it, as the thrush,
  perfectly singing, leaves all thought behind.

To that star-music all our song is speaking,
  to that nobility our saints forlorn,
and all our dreams no more than a sickle breaking
  in our hand, and all about us is the corn.

Yet with the harvest orb the silver car
  of the young moon is common in one growth,
so, if this earth be shadowy to that star,
  the single thought of beauty needs them both.

And builds with both, as surely as the arc
  of the moon's circle is the undrawn string,
as surely as the first note of the lark
  has all the substance of an English spring.

And thus to me may cleave the golden ghost,
  as I to him in the thought pointing on
to where, beyond us both, the poet lost
  on earth has found his bays in Avalon.

Humbert Wolfe

GOD'S LITTLE MOUNTAIN

Below, the river scrambled like a goat
Dislodging stones. The mountain stamped its foot,
Shaking, as from a trance. And I was shut
With wads of sound into a sudden quiet.

I thought the thunder had unsettled heaven,
All was so still. And yet the sky was cloven
By flame that left the air cold and engraven.
I waited for the word that was not given,

Pent up into a region of pure force,
Made subject to the pressure of the stars;
I saw the angels lifted like pale straws;
I could not stand before those winnowing eyes

And fell, until I found the world again.
Now I lack grace to tell what I have seen;
For though the head frames words the tongue has none,
And who will prove the surgeon to this stone?

Geoffrey Hill

THE ECSTASY

Long had we crept in cryptic
Delights and doubts on tiptoes,
The air growing purer, clearer
Continually; and nearer
We went on to the centre of
The garden, hand in hand, finger on lip.

On right and left uplifted
The fountains rose with swifter
And steadier urgence, argent
On steely pillars, larger
Each moment, spreading foamy plumes
Thinner and broader under blinding sun.

The air grows warmer; firmer
The silence grips it; murmur
Of insect buzz nor business
Or squirrel or bird there is not—
Only the flutter of the butterflies
Above the empty lawns, dance without noise.

So on we fared and forded
A brook with lilies bordered,
So cold it wrung with anguish
Bitterly our hearts. But language
Cannot at all make manifest
The quiet centre we found on the other side.

Never such a seal of silence
Did ice on streams or twilight
On birds impose. The pauses
In nature by her laws are
Imperfect; under the surface beats
A sound too constant to be ever observed.

From birth its stroke with equal
Dull rhythm, relentless sequence,
Taps on, unfelt, unaltered,
With beat that never falters—
Now known, like breathing, only when
It stopped. The permanent background failed our ear.

Said the voice of the garden, heard in
Our hearts, 'That was the burden
Of Time, his sombre drum-beat.
Here—oh hard to come by!—
True stillness dwells and will not change,
Never has changed, never begins nor ends.'

Who would not stay there, blither
Than memory knows? but either
Whisper of pride essayed us
Or meddling thought betrayed us,
Then shuddering doubt—oh suddenly
We were outside, back in the wavering world.

C. S. Lewis

Part IX

PATHS TO PEACE

HOLDING TO GOD

Lord, I am like to mistletoe,
Which has no root and cannot grow
Or prosper, but by that same tree
It clings about: so I by thee.
What need I then to fear at all
So long as I about thee crawl?
But if that tree should fall and die,
Tumble shall heaven, and so down will I.

Robert Herrick

For modes of faith let graceless Zealots fight;
He can't be wrong whose life is in the right;
In faith and hope the world will disagree,
But all mankind's concern is charity:
All must be false that thwart this one great end:
And all of God that bless mankind, or mend.
Man, like the generous vine, supported lives:
The strength he gains is from the embrace he gives.

Alexander Pope

PENITENCE

Oh! for a closer walk with GOD,
    A calm and heav'nly frame;
A light to shine upon the road
    That leads me to the Lamb!

Where is the blessedness I knew
    When first I saw the Lord?

Where is the soul-refreshing view
  of JESUS, and his word?

What peaceful hours I once enjoy'd!
  How sweet their mem'ry still!
But they have left an aching void,
  The world can never fill.

Return, O holy Dove, return,
  Sweet messenger of rest;
I hate the sins that made thee mourn,
  And drove thee from my breast.

The dearest idol I have known,
  Whate'er that idol be;
Help me to tear it from thy throne,
  And worship only thee.

So shall my walk be close with GOD,
  Calm and serene my frame;
So purer light shall mark the road
  That leads me to the Lamb.

William Cowper

I asked for Peace—
  My sins arose,
  And bound me close,
I could not find release.

I asked for Truth—
  My doubts came in,
  And with their din
They wearied all my youth.

I asked for Love—
  My lovers failed,
  And griefs assailed
Around, beneath, above.

I asked for Thee—
    And thou didst come
    To take me home
Within Thy Heart to be.

D. M. Dolben

Ye that do your Master's will,
Meek in heart be meeker still:
Day by day your sins confess,
Ye that walk in righteousness:
Gracious souls in grace abound,
Seek the Lord, whom ye have found.

He that comforts all that mourn
Shall to joy your sorrow turn:
Joy to know your sins forgiven,
Joy to keep the way to heaven,
Joy to win his welcome grace,
Joy to see Him face to face.

Charles Wesley

Once he had seen his sin as a thing that clung close as his shadow clung to his heels; now he knew that it was the very stuff of his soul. Never could he, a leaking bucket not to be mended, retain God's saving Grace, however freely outpoured. Never could he, that heavy lump of sin, do any other than sink, and sink again, however often Christ, walking on the waves, should stretch His hand to lift and bring him safe.

He did not know that though the bucket be leaky it matters not at all when it is deep in the deep sea, and the water both without it and within. He did not know, because he was too proud to know, that a man must endure to sink, and sink again, but always crying upon God, never for shame ceasing to cry, until the day when he shall find himself lifted by the bland swell of that power, inward, secret, as little to be known as to be doubted, the power of omnipotent grace in tranquil irresistible operation.

H. F. M. Prescott from The Man on a Donkey

I struck the board, and cry'd, 'No more,
        I will abroad.'
    What, shall I ever sigh and pine?
My lines and life are free; free as the road,
    Loose as the wind, as large as store.
        Shall I be still in suit?
    Have I no harvest but a thorn
    To let me bleed, and not restore
    What I have lost with cordial fruit?
        Sure there was wine
    Before my sighs did dry it; there was corn
        Before my tears did drown it;
    Is the year only lost to me?
        Have I no bays to crown it?
No flowers, no garlands gay? all blasted,
        All wasted?
    Not so, my heart; but there is fruit,
        And thou hast hands.
    Recover all thy sigh-blown age
On double pleasures; leave thy cold dispute
Of what is fit and not; forsake thy cage,
        Thy rope of sands
Which petty thoughts have made: and made to thee
    Good cable, to enforce and draw,
        And be thy law,
    While thou didst wink and wouldst not see.
        Away: take heed:
        I will abroad.
Call in thy death's head there, tie up thy fears.
        He that forbears
    To suit and serve his need
        Deserves his load.
But as I rav'd and grew more fierce and wild
        At every word,
    Methought I heard one calling, 'Child':
        And I replied, 'My Lord'.

George Herbert

HEAVEN HAVEN

The times are nightfall, look, their light grows less;
The times are winter, watch, a world undone:
They waste, they wither worse; they as they run
Or bring more or more blazon man's distress.

And I not help. Nor word now of success:
All is from wreck, here, there, to rescue one—
Work which to see scarce so much as begun
Makes welcome death, does dear forgetfulness.

Or what is else? There is your world within.
There rid the dragons, root out there the sin.
Your will in that small commonweal . . .

Gerard Manley Hopkins

TO HIS HEART BIDDING IT HAVE NO FEAR
(*Courage*)

Be you still, trembling heart;
Remember the wisdom out of the old days:
Him who trembles before the flame and the flood,
And the winds that blow through the starry ways,
Let the starry winds and the flame and the flood
Cover over and hide, for he has no part
With the lonely, majestical multitude.

W. B. Yeats

O heart, hold thee secure,
In this blind hour of stress,
Live on, love on, endure,
Uncowed, though comfortless.

Life's a wondrous thing
It seemed in bygone peace,
Though woe now jar the string
And all its music cease.

Even if thine own self have
No haven for defence;
Stand not the unshaken brave
To give thee confidence?

Worse than all worst 'twould be
If thou, who art thine all,
Shatter ev'n their reality
In thy poor fall.

Walter de la Mare

Saints and heroes, you dare say,
Like unicorns, have had their day.
Unlaurel the compulsive tough!
All pierced feet are feet of clay.

Envy—and paucity—of what
Men lived by to enlarge their lot,
Diminishing your share in them,
Downgrade you and not the great.

The saint falls down, the hero's treed
Often, we know it. Still we need
The vision that keeps burning from
Saintly trust, heroic deed.

Accept the flawed self, but aspire
To flights beyond it: wiser far
Lifting our eyes unto the hills
Than lowering them to sift the mire.
C. Day Lewis   from The Room and other poems

POSTURING

(*Loss of Self*)

Because of endless pride
Reborn with endless error
Each hour I look aside
Upon my secret mirror
Trying all postures there
To make my image fair.
Thou givest grapes, and I,
Though starving, turn to see
How dark the cool globes lie
In the white hand of me,
And linger gazing thither
Till the live clusters wither.

So should I quickly die
Narcissus-like of want,
But, in the glass, my eye
Catches such forms as haunt
Beyond nightmare, and make
Pride humble for pride's sake.

Then and then only turning
The stiff neck round, I grow
A molten man all burning
And look behind and know
Who made the glass, whose light makes
   dark, whose fair
Makes foul, my shadowy form reflected there
That self-Love, brought to bed of Love
   may die and bear
Her sweet son in despair.

C. S. Lewis

I walk these many rooms, wishing to trace
My frayed identity. In each, a ghost
Looks up and claims me for his long-lost brother—
Each unfamiliar, though he wears my face.
A draught of memory whispers I was most
Purely myself when I became another:

Tending a sick child, groping my way into
A woman's heart, lost in a poem, a cause,
I touched the marrow of my being, unbared
Through self-oblivion. Nothing remains so true
As the outgoingness. This moving house
Is home, and my home, only when it's shared.

C. Day Lewis

From far, from eve and morning
   And yon twelve-winded sky,
The stuff of life to knit me
   Blew hither: here am I.

Now—for a breath I tarry
   Nor yet disperse apart—
Take my hand quick and tell me
   What have you in your heart.

Speak now, and I will answer;
   How shall I help you, say;
Ere to the wind's twelve quarters
   I take my endless way.

A. E. Housman

THE CONFIDENCE

(Love)

After that moment when at last you let
The whole thing out, the grievances, the fear,
Did you then find it all could disappear,
Clothed in the kindly words 'Forgive, forget'?

It was not so. You only felt the shame
Of being caught out in a hopeless hour,
Of being once again within men's power,
A pawn, a puppet in a grown-up game.

Yet if you loved them and if they loved you
Beyond the carefully chosen words, the wide
Disarming land where terror seemed to hide
But could not, would the older wish come true?

Elizabeth Jennings

. . . Love will teach us all things: but we must learn how to win love; it is got with difficulty: it is a possession dearly bought with much labour and in a long time; for one must love not sometimes only, for a passing moment, but always. There is no man who doth not sometimes love: even the wicked can do that.

And let not men's sin dishearten thee: love a man even in his sin, for that love is a likeness of the divine love, and is the summit of love on earth. Love all God's creation, both the whole and every grain of sand. Love every leaf, every ray of light. Love the animals, love the plants, love each separate thing. If thou love each thing thou wilt perceive the mystery of God in all; and when once thou perceive this, thou wilt thenceforward grow every day to a fuller understanding of it: until thou come at last to love the whole world with a love that will then be all-embracing and universal.

Dostoevsky from Father Zossima's discourse in
'The Brothers Karamazof'

Is there not much more mystery in the relations of man to man then we generally recognize? None of us can truly assert that he really knows someone else, even if he has lived with him for years. Of that which constitutes our inner life we can impart even to those most intimate with us only fragments; the whole of it we cannot give nor would they be able to comprehend it. We wander through life together in a semi-darkness in which none of us can distinguish exactly the features of his neighbour; only from time to time, through some experience that we have of our companion, or through some remark that he passes he stands for a moment close to us, as though illumined by a flash of lightning. Then we see him as he really is. After that we again walk on together in the darkness, perhaps for a long time, and try in vain to make out our fellow-traveller's features.

To this fact, that we are each a secret to the other, we have to reconcile ourselves. To know one another cannot mean to know everything about each other; it means to feel mutual affection and confidence, and to believe in one another. To analyse others—unless it be to help back to a sound mind someone who is in spiritual or intellectual confusion—is a rude commencement, for there is a modesty of soul which we must recognize, just as we do that of the body. The soul, too, has its clothing of which we must not deprive it, and no one has a right to say to another: 'Because we belong to each other as we do, I have a right to know all your thoughts.' . . . In this matter giving is the only valuable process; it is only giving that stimulates. Impart as much as you can of your spiritual being to those who are on the road with you, and accept as something precious what comes back to you from them. . . . Only those who respect the personality of others can be of real use to them.

I think, therefore, that no one should compel himself to show to others more of his inner life than he feels it natural to show. We can do no more than let others judge for themselves what we inwardly and really are, and do the same ourselves with them. The one essential thing is that we strive to have light in ourselves. Our strivings will be recognized by others, and when people have light in themselves, it will shine out from them. Then we get to know each other as we walk together in the darkness, without needing to pass our hands over each other's faces, or to intrude into each other's hearts.

Albert Schweitzer from Memoirs of Childhood and Youth

PRAYER

And slowly answer'd Arthur from the barge:
'The old order changeth, yielding place to new,
And God fulfils himself in many ways,
Lest one good custom should corrupt the world.
Comfort thyself: what comfort is in me?
I have lived my life, and that which I have done
May He within himself make pure! but thou,
If thou shouldst never see my face again,
Pray for my soul. More things are wrought by prayer
Than this world dreams of. Wherefore, let thy voice
Rise like a fountain for me night and day.
For what are men better than sheep or goats
That nourish a blind life within the brain,
If, knowing God, they lift not hands of prayer
Both for themselves and those who call them friend?
For so the whole round earth is every way
Bound by gold chains about the feet of God.
But now farewell. I am going a long way
With these thou seëst—if indeed I go
(For all my mind is clouded with a doubt)—
To the island-valley of Avilion;
Where falls not hail, or rain, or any snow,
Nor ever wind blows loudly; but it lies
Deep-meadow'd, happy, fair with orchard lawns
And bowery hollows crown'd with summer sea,
Where I will heal me of my grievous wound.'

Lord Tennyson   from Morte d'Arthur

THE BELFRY

I have seen it standing up grey.
Gaunt, as though no sunlight
Could ever thaw out the music
Of its great bell; terrible
In its own way, for religion
Is like that. There are times

When a bleak frost is upon
One's whole being, and the heart
In its bone belfry hangs and is dumb.
But who is to know? Always,
Even in winter in the cold
Of a stone church, on his knees
Someone is praying, whose prayers fall
Steadily through the hard spell
Of weather that is between God
And himself. Perhaps they are warm rain
That brings the sun and afterwards flowers
On the raw graves and throbbing of bells.

R. S. Thomas

PATIENCE

When shall I enjoy a solid peace, a peace never to be disturbed and always secure, a peace within and without, a peace every way assured? . . .

As long as we carry about this frail body, we cannot be without sin, nor live without weariness and sorrow.

We would fain be at rest from all misery; but because we have lost innocence by sin, we have lost also true blessedness

We must therefore maintain patience, and wait for the mercy of God, until iniquity pass away; and this mortality be swallowed up of life. . . .

Peace shall come in the day which is known unto the Lord and it will not be day or night, such as is at present, but everlasting light, infinite brightness, steadfast peace, and secure rest . . . because after winter comes summer, after night the day returns, after a storm there follows a great calm.

Thomas à Kempis from 'The Imitation of Christ

PART X

WISDOM OF THE MEN OF PEACE

THE TWIN-VERSES

All that we are is the result of what we have thought: it is founded on our thoughts, it is made up of our thoughts. If a man speaks or acts with evil thought, pain follows him, as the wheel follows the foot of the ox that draws the carriage.

All that we are is the result of what we have thought: it is founded on our thoughts, it is made up of our thoughts. If a man speaks or acts with a pure thought, happiness follows him, like a shadow that never leaves him.

'He abused me, he beat me, he defeated me, he robbed me'— in those who harbour such thoughts hatred will never cease.

For hatred does not cease by hatred at any time: hatred ceases by love—this is an old rule.

The world does not know that we must all come to an end here; but those who know it, their quarrels cease at once.

Gotama Buddha   563-483 B.C.

THE SERMON ON ABUSE

And the Blessed One observed the ways of society and noticed how much misery came from malignity and foolish offences done only to gratify vanity and self-seeking pride.

And the Buddha said: 'If a man foolishly does me wrong, I will return to him the protection of my ungrudging love; the more evil comes from him the more good shall go from me; the fragrance of goodness always comes to me, and the harmful air of evil goes to him.'

A foolish man learning that the Buddha observed the principle of great love which commends the return of good for evil, came and abused him. The Buddha was silent, pitying his folly.

When the man had finished his abuse, the Buddha asked him, saying: 'Son, if a man declined to accept a present made to him, to whom would it belong?' And he answered: 'In that

197

case it would belong to the man who offered it.'

'My son,' said the Buddha, 'thou hast railed at me, but I decline to accept thy abuse, and request thee to keep it thyself. Will it not be a source of misery to thee? As the echo belongs to the sound, and the shadow to the substance, so misery will overtake the evil-doer without fail.'

The abuser made no reply, and Buddha continued:

'A wicked man who reproaches a virtuous one is like one who looks up and spits at heaven; the spittle soils not the heaven, but comes back and defiles his own person.

'The slanderer is like one who flings dust at another when the wind is contrary; the dust does but return on him who threw it. The virtuous man cannot be hurt and the misery that the other would inflict comes back on himself.'

The abuser went away ashamed, but he came again and took refuge in the Buddha, the Dharma, and the Sangha.

Gotama Buddha   563-483 B.C.

UNIVERSAL LOVE

When all the people in the world love one another, then the strong will not overpower the weak, the many will not oppress the few, the wealthy will not mock the poor, the honoured will not disdain the humble, and the cunning will not deceive the simple. And it is all due to mutual love that calamities, strifes, complaints, and hatred are prevented from arising. Therefore the benevolent exalt it.

But the gentlemen of the world would say: 'So far so good. It is of course very excellent when love becomes universal. But it is only a difficult and distant ideal.'

Motsi said: This is simply because the gentlemen of the world do not recognize what is to the benefit of the world, or understand what is its calamity. Now, to besiege a city, to fight in the fields, or to achieve a name at the cost of death—these are what men find difficult. Yet when the superior encourages them, the multitudes can do them. Besides, universal love and mutual aid is quite different from these. Whoever loves others is loved by others; whoever benefits others is benefited by others; whoever

198

hates others is hated by others; whoever injured others is injured by others. Then, what difficulty is there with it (universal love)? Only, the ruler fails to embody it in his government and the ordinary man in his conduct.

Motsi (or Noti) 463-401 B.C.

CONDEMNATION OF OFFENSIVE WAR

Now, about a country going to war. If it is winter it will be too cold, if in summer it will be too hot. So it should be neither in winter nor in summer. If it is in spring it will take people away from mowing and planting; if it is autumn it will take people away from reaping and harvesting. Should they be taken away in either of these seasons, innumerable people would die of hunger and cold. And, when the army sets out, the bamboo arrows, the feather flags, the house tents, the armour, the shields, the sword hilts—innumerable quantities of these will break and rot and never come back. The spears, the lances, the swords, the paniards, the chariots, the carts—innumerable quantities of these will break and rot and never come back. Then innumerable horses and oxen will start out fat and come back lean or will not return at all. And innumerable people will die because their food will be cut off and cannot be supplied on account of the great distances of the roads. And innumerable people will be sick and die of the constant danger and the irregularity of eating and drinking and the extremes of hunger and over-eating. Then, the army will be lost in large numbers or entirely; in either case the number will be innumerable. And this means the spirits will lose their worshippers, and the number of these will also be innumerable.

Such an undertaking is not in accordance with the interest of the country. . . .

Motsi (or Noti) 463-401 B.C.

To us, glorying as we do in the name of Christ, who taught

nothing by his precept, and exhibited nothing in his example, but mildness and gentleness, who are members of one body, all of us one flesh, who grow in grace by one and the same spirit; who are fed by the same sacrament; who adhere to the same head; who are called to the same immortality; who hope for a sublime communion with God, that as Christ and the Father are one, so also may we be one with him; can any thing in this world be of such value as to provoke us to war? A state so destructive, so hideous, and so base, that even when it is founded on a just cause, it can never be pleasing to a good man.

In war, he who conquers weeps over his triumph. War draws such a troop of evil in its train, that the poets find reason for the fiction which relates, that war was brought from hell to earth by a deputation of devils.

Erasmus   Extract from a letter to the Abbot of St. Bertin

Now the time of my commitment to the house of correction being nearly ended, and there being many new soldiers raised, the commissioners would have made me captain over them, and the soldiers said they would have none but me. So the keeper of the house of correction was commanded to bring me before the commissioners and soldiers in the market-place; and there they offered me that preferment, as they called it, asking me, if I would not take up arms for the Commonwealth against Charles Stuart? I told them, I knew from whence all wars arose, even from lust, according to James's doctrine; and that I lived in the virtue of that life and power that took away the occasion of all wars. But they courted me to accept their offer, and thought I did but compliment them. But I told them, I was come into the covenant of peace, which was before wars and strife were. They said, they offered it in love and kindness to me, because of my virtue; and such like flattering words they used. But I told them, if that was their love and kindness, I trampled it under my feet. Then their rage got up, and they said, 'Take him away, jailer, and put him into the dungeon amongst the rogues and felons.' So I was had away and put into a lousy, stinking place, without any bed, amongst thirty felons, where I was kept almost half a year, unless it were at times; for they would sometimes let me walk in the garden, having a belief that I would not go away. Now when they had got me into Derby dungeon it was the belief and saying of the people that I should never come out; but I had faith in God, and believed I should be delivered in his time; for the Lord had said to me before, that I was not to be removed from the place yet, being set there for a service which he had for me to do. . . .

. . . All that pretend to fight for Christ, are deceived; for his kingdom is not of this world, therefore his servants do not fight. Fighters are not of Christ's kingdom, but are without Christ's kingdom; his kingdom starts in peace and righteousness, but fighters are in the lust, and all that would destroy men's lives, are not of Christ's mind, who came to save men's lives. Christ's kingdom is not of this world; it is peaceable; and all that are in strife, are not of his kingdom . . . All such as pretend Christ Jesus, and confess him, and yet run into the use of carnal weapons, wrestling with flesh and blood, throw away the spiritual weapons. They that would be wrestlers with flesh and blood, throw away Christ's doctrine; the flesh is got up in them, and they are weary of their sufferings. Such as would revenge themselves, are out of Christ's doctrine. Such as being stricken on one cheek, would not turn the other, are out of Christ's doctrine: and such as do not love one another, nor love enemies, are out of Christ's doctrine. . . .

George Fox   from his Journal

LOVING KINDNESS

. . . And surely it is not a vain dream that man shall come to find his joys only in acts of enlightenment and of mercy, and not in cruel pleasures, as he doth now, in gluttony, lust, pride, boasting and envious selfexaltation. I hold firmly that this is no dream but that the time is at hand . . . I believe that through Christ we shall accomplish this great work . . . and all men will say 'The stone which the builders rejected is become the chief stone of the corner.' And of the mockers themselves we may ask, If this faith of ours be a dream, then how long is it to wait ere ye shall have finished your edifice, and have ordered everything justly by the intellect alone without Christ? . . . In truth they have a greater faculty for dreaming than we have. They think to order all wisely; but, having rejected Christ, they will end by drenching the world with blood. For blood crieth again for blood, and they that take the sword shall perish by the sword.

Dostoevsky   from Father Zossima's discourse in 'The Brothers Karamazof'

I am not a visionary. I claim to be a practical idealist. The religion of non-violence is not meant merely for the Rishis and saints. It is meant for the common people as well. Non-violence is the law of our species as violence is the law of the brute. The spirit lies dormant in the brute and he knows no law but that of physical might. The dignity of man requires obedience to a higher law—to the strength of the spirit.

I have therefore ventured to place before India the ancient law of self-sacrifice. For Satyagraha and its off-shoots, non-co-operation and civil disobedience, are nothing but new names for the law of suffering. The Rishis, who discovered the law of non-violence in the midst of violence, were greater geniuses than Newton. They were themselves greater warriors than Wellington. Having themselves known the use of arms, they realized their uselessness and taught a weary world that its salvation lay not through violence but through non-violence.

Non-violence in its dynamic condition means conscious suffering. It does not mean meek submission to the will of the evil-doer, but it means the putting of one's whole soul against the will of the tyrant. Working under this law of our being, it is possible for a single individual to defy the whole might of an unjust empire to save his honour, his religion, his soul and lay the foundation for that empire's fall or its regeneration.

And so I am not pleading for India to practise non-violence, because it is weak. I want her to practise non-violence being conscious of her strength and power. No training in arms is required for realization of her strength. We seem to need it, because we seem to think that we are but a lump of flesh. I want India to recognize that she has a soul that cannot perish and that can rise triumphant above every physical weakness and defy the physical combination of a whole world. What is the meaning of Rama, a mere human being, with his host of monkeys, pitting himself against the insolent strength of ten-headed Ravan surrounded in supposed safety by the raging water on all sides of Lanka? Does it not mean the conquest of physical might by spiritual strength? However, being a practical man, I do not wait till India recognizes the practicability of the spiritual life in the political world. India considers herself to be powerless and paralysed before the machine-guns, the tanks and the aeroplanes of the English. And she takes up Non-co-operation out of her weakness. It must still serve the same purpose, namely, bring her delivery from the crushing weight of British injustice, if a sufficient number of people practise it.

Mohandas K. Gandhi

Police rushed upon the advancing marchers and rained blows on their heads with their steel-shod lathis. Not one of the marchers even raised an arm to fend off the blows. . . . Those struck down fell sprawling, unconscious or writhing in pain with fractured skulls or broken shoulders. In two or three minutes the ground was quilted with bodies. Great patches of blood widened on their white clothes. The survivors without breaking ranks silently and doggedly marched on until struck down. . . .

Then another column formed while the leaders pleaded with them to retain their self-control. They marched slowly towards the police. Although every one knew that within a few minutes he would be beaten down, perhaps killed, I could detect no signs of wavering or fear. They marched steadily with heads up, without the encouragement of music or cheering or any possibility that they might escape injury or death. The police rushed out and methodically and mechanically beat down the second column. There was no fight, no struggle; the marchers simply walked forward until struck down.

(*A description by Webb Millar of The Salt March, undertaken by Gandhi's disciples at a time when he was in jail*)

A non-violent man can do nothing save by the power and grace of God. Without it he won't have the courage to die without anger, without fear and without retaliation. Such courage comes from the belief that God sits in the heart of all, and that there should be no fear in the presence of God.

I am a man of peace. I believe in peace. But I do not want peace at any price. I do not want the peace that you find in stone; I do not want the peace that you find in the grave; but I do want the peace which you find embedded in the human breast, which is exposed to the arrows of the whole world, but which is protected from all harm by the power of Almighty God.

Mahatma Gandhi

In the evenings, after praying with his mother, he would add his own silent prayer for all living creatures: 'Dear God, protect and bless all things that breathe, guard them from all evil and let them sleep in peace.'

Sometimes the fact of pain shocked him into violent and repeated resolves to so order his life that he would inflict no pain on anything that lived and breathed. . . . When he was seven or eight he went out bird-hunting with a friend. Like his friend, he was armed with a catapult. At the moment when young Schweitzer stooped to gather a stone to insert in the catapult, the Easter bells rang out. It was like a sign from heaven. He began to shout and wave his arms, shooing the birds away, then he fled home. He had discovered the commandment that was to weigh increasingly on him over the years: 'Thou shalt not kill.' . . .

Ehrfurcht vor dem Leben. Reverence for Life. *Ehrfurcht* means more than 'reverence'. It has overtones of awe and shuddering wonder, and great blessedness. Before God a man may abase himself in holy awe. A man may humble himself before the infinite spaces of the firmament. So should a man humble himself before the ever-present miracle of life. Let him regard the miracle with reverential fear and wonder, and let him never cease regarding it in this way, for all life is the vehicle of the power of God. . . .

A man who possesses an entire veneration and awe of life

will not simply say his prayers: he will throw himself into the battle to preserve life, if for no other reason than that he is himself an extension of the life around him, life being so holy and every man being part of this holiness. A man rejoicing in that veneration for life is therefore led 'into an unrest such as the world does not know, but he obtains from it a blessedness which the world cannot give'. And if his task is harder, because he assumes such huge responsibilities, the rewards are greater, for those who help to preserve life and heal wounds and diminish pain come to know the deepest happiness known to men.

G. Robert Payne   from Schweitzer Hero of Africa

Man has become a superman, and suffers from a fatal imperfection of the spirit. He is not raised to a superhuman level of understanding which corresponds to the possession of superhuman strength. He lacks the capacity to put his gigantic power to work for rational and useful ends; instead he puts his power to work for destruction and murderous ends. So it happens that the advance of science, instead of being advantageous to him, has proved fatal to him. . . .

Only now does the full horror of our position become clear to us. We can no longer evade the problem of the future of mankind. The essential fact should now strike home to us (and it should have struck home long ago) that inhumanity is the constant companion of the superman, and progresses as he progresses. We have tolerated the mass killings of men in time of war, . . . the annihilation by atomic bombing of whole cities and their populations . . . and the transformation of men into living torches. We have learned of these things by radio or from the newspapers, and we have judged them according to whether they signify achievements accomplished by the society we belong to, or whether they were done by our enemies. When we admit that all these things are direct results of acts of inhumanity, we qualify the admission that 'war is war', and there is nothing we can do about it. So, by offering no resistance and by resigning ourselves, we become guilty of a crime against humanity.

The important thing is that all of us should acknowledge that we are guilty of inhumanity. The horror of the avowal must arouse us from our torpor, and compel us to hope and work for an age when there will be no war. These hopes, these determinations, can have only one object: the attainment, through the growth of the spirit, of a state of superior reason in which we shall no longer put to deathly uses the vast powers which now lie at our disposal.

Albert Schweitzer   from the Nobel Prize Speech

I am no doctrinaire pacifist. I have tried to embrace a realistic pacifism. Moreover, I see the pacifist position not as sinless but as the lesser evil in the circumstances. Therefore I do not claim to be free from the moral dilemmas that the Christian non-pacifist confronts. But I am convinced that the church cannot remain silent while mankind faces the threat of being plunged into the abyss of nuclear annihilation. If the church is true to its mission it must call for an end to the arms race.

In recent months I have also become more and more convinced of the reality of a personal God. True, I have always believed in the personality of God. But in past years the idea of a personal God was little more than a metaphysical category which I found theologically and philosophically satisfying. Now it is a living reality that has been validated in the experiences of everyday life. Perhaps the suffering, frustration and agonizing moments which I have had to undergo occasionally as a result of my involvement in a difficult struggle have drawn me closer to God. Whatever the cause, God has been profoundly real to me in recent months. In the midst of outer dangers I have felt an inner calm and known resources of strength that only God could give. In many instances I have felt the power of God transforming the fatigue of despair into the buoyancy of hope. I am convinced that the universe is under the control of a loving purpose and that in the struggle for righteousness man has cosmic companionship. Behind the harsh appearances of the world there is a benign power. To say God is personal is not to make him an object among other objects or attribute to him the finiteness and limitations of human personality; it is to take what is finest and noblest in our consciousness and affirm its perfect existence in him. It is certainly true that human personality is limited, but personality as such involves no necessary limitations. It simply means self-consciousness and self-direction. So in the truest sense of the word, God is a living God. In him there is feeling and will, responsive to the deepest yearnings of the human heart: this God both evokes and answers prayers.

The past decade has been a most exciting one. In spite of the tensions and uncertainties of our age something profoundly meaningful has begun. Old systems of exploitation and oppression are passing away and new systems of justice and equality are being born. In a real sense ours is a great time in which to be alive. Therefore I am not yet discouraged about the future. Granted that the easygoing optimism of yesterday is impossible. Granted that we face a world crisis which often leaves us standing amid the surging murmur of life's restless sea. But every crisis has both its dangers and its opportunities. Each can spell either salvation or doom. In a dark, confused world the spirit of God may yet reign supreme.

Martin Luther King

SUFFERING AND FAITH

Some of my personal sufferings over the last few years have also served to shape my thinking. I always hesitate to mention these circumstances for fear of conveying the wrong impression. A person who constantly calls attention to his trials and sufferings is in danger of developing a martyr complex and of making others feel that he is consciously seeking sympathy. It is possible for one to be self-centred in his self-denial and self-righteous in his self-sacrifice. But I feel somewhat justified in mentioning them in this article because of the influence they have had in shaping my thinking.

Due to my involvement in the struggle for the freedom of my people, I have known very few quiet days in the last few years. I have been arrested five times and put in Alabama jails. My home has been bombed twice. A day seldom passes that my family and I are not the recipients of threats of death. I have been the victim of a near-fatal stabbing. So in a real sense I have been battered by the storms of persecution. I must admit that at times I have felt that I could no longer bear such a heavy burden, and have been tempted to retreat to a more quiet and serene life. But every time such a temptation appeared, something came to strengthen and sustain my determination. I have learned now that the Master's burden is light precisely when we take his yoke upon us.

My personal trials have also taught me the value of unmerited suffering. As my sufferings mounted I soon realized that there were two ways that I could respond to my situation: either to react with bitterness or seek to transform the suffering into a creative force. Recognizing the necessity for suffering I have tried to make of it a virtue. If only to save myself from bitterness, I have attempted to see my personal ordeals as an opportunity to transform myself and heal the people involved in the tragic situation which now obtains. I have lived these last few years with the conviction that unearned suffering is redemptive.

There are some who still find the cross a stumbling block, and others consider it foolishness, but I am more convinced than ever before that it is the power of God unto social and individual salvation. So like Apostle Paul I can now humbly yet proudly say, 'I bear in my body the marks of the Lord Jesus.' The suffering and agonizing moments through which I have passed over the last few years have also drawn me closer to God. More than ever before I am convinced of the reality of a personal God.

Martin Luther King

There are certain things that our age needs, and certain things it should avoid. It needs compassion, and a wish that mankind should be happy: it needs the desire for knowledge and the determination to eschew pleasant myths; it needs, above all, courageous hope and the impulse to creativeness. . . . The root of the matter is a very simple and old-fashioned thing, a thing so simple that I am almost ashamed to mention it for fear of the derisive smile with which wise cynics will greet my words. The thing I mean—please forgive me for mentioning it—is love, Christian love, or compassion. If you feel this, you have a motive for existence, a guide in action, a reason for courage, an imperative necessity for intellectual honesty.

Bertrand Russell   from Impact of Science on Society

Part XI

WAR

THE PARABLE OF THE OLD MEN AND THE YOUNG

So Abram rose, and clave the wood, and went,
And took the fire with him, and a knife.
And as they journeyed both of them together,
Isaac the first-born spake and said, My Father,
Behold the preparations, fire and iron,
But where the lamb for this burnt-offering?
Then Abram bound the youth with belts and straps,
And builded parapets and trenches there,
And stretched forth the knife to slay his son.
When lo! an angel called him out of heaven,
Saying, Lay not thy hand upon the lad,
Neither do anything to him. Behold,
A ram, caught in a thicket by its horns;
Offer the Ram of Pride instead of him.
But the old man would not so, but slew his son,—
And half the seed of Europe, one by one.

Wilfred Owen

EXPOSURE

Our brains ache, in the merciless iced east winds that knive
     us . . .
Wearied we keep awake because the night is silent . . .
Low drooping flares confuse our memory of the salient . . .
Worried by silence, sentries whisper, curious, nervous,
          But nothing happens.

Watching, we hear the mad gusts tugging on the wire,
Like twitching agonies of men among its brambles.
Northward, incessantly, the flickering gunnery rumbles,
Far off, like a dull rumour of some other war.
          What are we doing here?

The poignant misery of dawn begins to grow . . .
We only know war lasts, rain soaks, and clouds sag stormy.
Dawn massing in the east her melancholy army
Attacks once more in ranks on shimmering ranks of grey,
    But nothing happens.

Sudden successive flights of bullets streak the silence.
Less deadly than the air that shudders black with snow,
With sidelong flowing flakes that flock, pause, and renew,
We watch them wandering up and down the wind's
   nonchalance,
    But nothing happens.

Pale flakes with fingering stealth come feeling for our faces—
We cringe in holes, back on forgotten dreams, and stare, snow-
   dazed,
Deep into grassier ditches. So we drowse, sun-dozed,
Littered with blossoms trickling where the blackbird fusses.
    Is it that we are dying?

Slowly our ghosts drag home: glimpsing the sunk fires, glozed
With crusted dark-red jewels; crickets jingle there;
For hours the innocent mice rejoice: the house is theirs;
Shutters and doors, all closed: on us the doors are closed,—
    We turn back to our dying.

Since we believe not otherwise can kind fires burn;
Nor ever suns smile true on child, or field, or fruit.
For God's invincible spring our love is made afraid;
Therefore, not loath, we lie out here; therefore were born,
    For love of God seems dying.

To-night, His frost will fasten on this mud and us,
Shrivelling many hands, puckering foreheads crisp.
The burying-party, picks and shovels in their shaking grasp,
Pause over half-known faces. All their eyes are ice,
    But nothing happens.

Wilfred Owen

212

STRANGE MEETING

It seemed that out of battle I escaped
Down some profound dull tunnel long since scooped
Through granites which titanic wars had groined
Yet also there encumbered sleepers groaned.
Too fast in thought or death to be bestirred.
Then, as I probed them, one sprang up, and stared
With piteous recognition in fixed eyes,
Lifting distressful hands as if to bless.
And by his smile, I knew that sullen hall,
By his dead smile I knew we stood in Hell.
With a thousand pains that vision's face was grained;
Yet no blood reached there from the upper ground,
And no guns thumped, or down the flues made moan.
'Strange friend,' I said, 'here is no cause to mourn.'
'None,' said the other, 'save the undone years,
The hopelessness. Whatever hope is yours,
Was my life also; I went hunting wild
After the wildest beauty in the world,
Which lies not calm in eyes, or braided hair,
But mocks the steady running of the hour,
And if it grieves, grieves richlier than here.
For by my glee might many men have laughed,
And of my weeping something had been left,
Which must die now. I mean the truth untold,
The pity of war, the pity war distilled.
Now men will go content with what we spoiled.
Or, discontent, boil bloody, and be spilled.
They will be swift with swiftness of the tigress,
None will break ranks, though nations trek from progress.
Courage was mine, and I had mystery,
Wisdom was mine, and I had mastery;
To miss the march of this retreating world
Into vain citadels that are not walled.
Then, when much blood had clogged their chariot-wheels
I would go up and wash them from sweet wells,
Even with truths that lie too deep for taint.
I would have poured my spirit without stint
But not through wounds; not on the cess of war.
Foreheads of men have bled where no wounds were.

I am the enemy you killed, my friend.
I knew you in this dark; for so you frowned
Yesterday through me as you jabbed and killed.
I parried; but my hands were loath and cold.
Let us sleep now. . . .'

Wilfred Owen

AT THE BRITISH WAR CEMETERY, BAYEUX

I walked where in their talking graves
And shirts of earth five thousand lay,
When history with ten feasts of fire
Had eaten the red air away.

I am Christ's boy, I cried, I bear
In iron hands the bread, the fishes,
I hang with honey and with rose
This tidy wreck of all your wishes.

On your geometry of sleep
The chestnut and the fir-tree fly,
And lavender and marguerite
Forge with their flowers an English sky.

Turn now towards the belling town
Your jigsaws of impossible bone,
And rising read your rank of snow
Accurate as death upon the stone.

About your easy heads my prayers
I said with syllables of clay,
What gift, I asked, shall I bring now
Before I weep and walk away?

Take, they replied, the oak and laurel.
Take our fortune of tears and live
Like a spendthrift lover. All we ask
Is the one gift you cannot give.

Charles Causley

GRIEFS FOR DEAD SOLDIERS

I

Mightiest, like some universal cataclysm,
Will be the unveiling of their cenotaph:
The crowds will stand struck, like the painting of a terror
Where the approaching planet, a half-day off,
Hangs huge above the thin skulls of the silenced birds;
Each move, each sound, a fresh-out epitaph—
Monstrousness of the moment making the air stone.
Though thinly, the bugle will then cry,
The dead drum tap, and the feet of the columns
And the sergeant-major's voice blown about by the wind
Make these dead magnificent, their souls
Scrolled and supporting the sky, and the national sorrow,
Over the crowds that know of no other wound,
Permanent stupendous victory.

II

Secretest, tiniest, there, where the widow watches on the table
The telegram opening of its own accord
Inescapably and more terribly than any bomb
That dives to the cellar and lifts the house. The bared
Words shear the hawsers of love that now lash
Back in darkness, blinding and severing. To a world
Lonely as her skull and little as her heart.

The doors and windows open like great gates to a hell.
Still she will not carry cups from table to sink.
She cannot build her sorrow into a monument
And walk away from it. Closer than thinking
The dead man hangs around her neck, but never
Close enough to be touched, or thanked even,
For being all that remains in a world smashed.

III

Truest, and only just, here, where since
The battle passed the grass has sprung up
Surprisingly in the valleyful of dead men.
Under the blue sky heavy crow and black fly move.
Flowers bloom prettily to the edge of the mass grave

Where spades hack, and the diggers grunt and sweat.
Among the flowers the dead wait like brides

To surrender their limbs; thus of another body flung
Down, the jolted shape of a face, earth into the mouth—
Moment that could annihilate a watcher!
Cursing the sun that makes their work long
Or the black lively flies that bite their wrists,
The burial party works with a craftsman calm.
Weighing their grief by the ounce, and burying it.

Ted Hughes

FOR THE UNKNOWN SEAMEN OF THE 1939-45 WAR BURIED IN IONA CHURCHYARD

One would like to be able to write something for them
not for the sake of the writing but because
a man should be named in dying as well as living,
in drowning as well as on death-bed, and because
the brain being brain must try to establish laws.

Yet these events are not amenable
to any discipline that we can impose
and are not in the end even imaginable.
What happened was simply this, bad luck for those
who have lain here twelve years in a changing pose.

These things happen and there's no explaining,
and to call them 'chosen' might abuse a word.
It is better also not to assume a mourning,
moaning stance. These may well have concurred
in whatever suddenly struck them through the absurd

or maybe meaningful. One simply doesn't
know enough, or understand what came
out of the altering weather in a fashioned
descriptive phrase that was common to each name,
or maybe have surrounded each like a dear frame.

Best not to make much of it and leave these seamen
in the equally altering acre they now have
inherited from strangers though yet human.
They fell from sea to earth from grave to grave
and, griefless now, taught others how to grieve.

Iain Crichton Smith

THE PRISONER

Suppose that what's now sky and wind for you,
air for your mouth and brightness for your vision,
turned into stone all round that small provision
of space your heart and hands were welcome to.

And what's *to-morrow* in you now and *then*
and *later* and *next year* and *something waiting*
became all sore in you and suppurating
and festered on and never dawned again.

And what had become insane and raged
within you, and your mouth, so disengaged
from laughter, were now laughing long and hard.

And what had once been God were just your guard,
attempting with a dirty eye to fill
the last hole up. And yet you lived on still.

Rainer Maria Rilke

THE PRISONER
A Short Letter to the World

Gripped in a crossbow's teeth
I am held and cannot fly.

My soul is torn

by its struggle to break free
but I cannot pull out these bolts
that have been shot home through my breast. . . .

You do not know what a man is
torn and bleeding in a snare.
If you knew it you would come
on the waves and on the wind
out of every borderland
with your hearts melting and sick
holding up your fists aloft
come to rescue what is yours.

If one day you come too late
and you find my body cold,
if you find my comrades dead
white as snow among their chains,
pick our banners up again
and our anguish and our dreams
and the names upon the walls
which we carved with loving care. . . .

If one day you come too late
and you find my body cold
look among the lonely places
in the wall to find my will:
to the world I do bequeath
all I have and all I feel
all I was among my kind
all I am and all I stand for:
one banner that brings no sorrow
one love, a little verse . . .
and on the lacerating stones
of this grey yard which none will enter
my cry to stand like an appalling
scarlet statue in the centre.

Marcos Ana   A Political Prisoner who was in
Burgos Jail for twenty-two years

GHOSTS, FIRE, WATER

On the Hiroshima panels by Iri Maruki and Toshiko Alamatsu

These are the ghosts of the unwilling dead,
Grey ghosts of that imprinted flash of memory
Whose flaming and eternal instant haunts
The speechless dark with dread and anger.

Grey, out of pale nothingness their agony appears.
Like ash they are blown and blasted on the wind's
Vermilion breathlessness, like shapeless smoke
Their shapes are torn across the paper sky.

These scarred and ashen ghosts are quick
With pain's unutterable speech, their flame-cracked flesh
Writhes and is heavy as the worms, the bitter dirt;
Lonely as in death they bleed, naked as in birth.

They greet each other in a ghastly paradise,
These ghosts who cannot come with gifts and flowers.
Here they receive each other with disaster's common love,
Covering one another's pain with shrivelled hands.

They are not beautiful, yet beauty is in their truth.
There is no easy music in their silent screams,
No ordered dancing in their grief's distracted limbs.
Their shame is ours. We, too, are haunted by their fate.

In the shock of flame, their tears brand our flesh,
We twist in their furnace, and our scorching throats
Parch for the waters where the cool dead float.
We press our lips upon the river where they drink, and drown.

Their voices call to us, in pain and indignation:
'This is what you have done to us!'
—Their accusation is our final hope. Be comforted.
Yes, we have heard you, ghosts of our indifference,

We hear your cry, we understand your warnings.
We, too, shall refuse to accept our fate!

Haunt us with the truth of our betrayal
Until the earth's united voices shout refusal, sing your peace!

Forgive us, that we had to see your passion to remember
What we must never again deny: *Love one another.*

James Kirkup

THE LONG WAR

Less passionate the long war throws
its burning thorn about all men,
caught in one grief, we share one wound,
and cry one dialect of pain.

We have forgot who fired the house,
whose easy mischief spilt first blood,
under one raging roof we lie
the fault no longer understood.

But as our twisted arms embrace
the desert where our cities stood,
death's family likeness in each face
must show, at last, our brotherhood.

Laurie Lee

All the world over, nursing their scars,
Sit the old fighting-men broke in the wars—
Sit the old fighting men, surly and grim
Mocking the lilt of the conquerors' hymn.

Dust of the battle o'erwhelmed them and hid,
Fame never found them for aught that they did.
Wounded and spent to the lazar they drew,
Lining the road where the Legions roll through.

Sons of the Laurel who press to your meed,
(Worthy God's pity most—ye who succeed!)
Ere you go triumphing, crowned, to the stars,
Pity poor fighting men, broke in the wars!

Rudyard Kipling

FOR THE RECORD

What was your war record, Prytherch?
I know: up and down the same field,
Following a horse; no oil for tractors;
Sniped at by rain, but never starving.
Did you listen to the reports
Of how heroes are fashioned and how killed?
Did you wait up late for the news?
Your world was the same world as before
Wars were contested, noisier only
Because of the echoes in the sky.
The blast worried your hair on its way to the hill;
The distances were a wound
Opened each night. Yet in your acres,
With no medals to be won,
You were on the side of life,
Helping it in through the dark door
Of earth and beast, quietly repairing
The rents of history with your hands.

R. S. Thomas

POEM TO BE CAST INTO THE SEA
IN A BOTTLE

Friend, in place of dark red wine, receive
this poem bound in glass the colour of a drowning wave.
It is for you I write it, friend, with ceremonious cast
bestow its dry simplicity like a libation
on the sundering oceans of our time, while present, past

and future skies unite in one
with all calling birds falling in one voice
upon your distant loneliness, regardless of my choice.

Whether on crowded snows of ice-packed sand,
on rich coast or desert shore you stand,
this is the word I sent you, out of the illness
of the divided world; this plea,
cast out of storm into infinite calm, the stillness
of your look, your hand's assurances, warm across the sea.
My tongue seals like a cork heavy with wine
the drinking mouth, that our sorrow crusts with brine.

May you, friend, seize it in eager teeth,
and draw it gently out, drinking the sweetness underneath,
the sunlight that in waves of darkness mourns
for the freedom of a peaceful air, where trust
and sanity together breathe, and passion burns
with a regenerating flame upon the innocence we lost
in cities bright with pain below the neon heat,
in wars and prisons, wildernesses of consuming hate.

The world seems at its luckless end, if we
unknown, yet known to one another go.
There is no more durable catastrophe, if man,
sure in his heart of love, denies its name
and to its perfect grace prefers the wounds of scorn.
Look in your own heart when you read this rhyme,
and let these words upon your memory flow
like wine that lingers in the blood, speaking a tongue
we know.

James Kirkup

PRAYER

Peace, you were always there.
In the collapsing house you lived,
and built it as it fell.

The child without a head
smiled then for you alone; our lost
companions were found again.

You vanquished with a hush
the bomb that toppled out of tents
of light, and filled the ruin with a seed.
Captain and crew were drowned, but in your
stillness, a falling wave of stone whose one
opened window fell always where we stood.

Each disappearing street became
the road you walked along towards us all,
all prisoners until your sentence of release.
You came with pardon, and there was no enemy
that did not give his life for you
in natural surrender, forgiven by a word.

When will the simple dove return, the bird
bearing the seed of our transfiguration?
O, peace, come with the sun, and help us to connect
the winters of the living world.
O let us love hard the life we cannot hate!
Come, peace, come not too late.

James Kirkup

THE HARROWING OF HELL

'After sharp showers,' said Peace, 'how shining the sun!
There's no weather warmer, than after watery clouds.
Nor any love that has more delight, nor friendship fonder,
Than after war and woe, when Love and Peace are the masters.
Never was war in this world, nor wickedness so cruel,
But that Love, if he liked, could bring all to laughing,
And Peace, through patience, put stop to all perils.'

William Langland

PART XII

ACCEPTANCE

THE HEART'S DESIRE IS FULL OF SLEEP

The heart's desire is full of sleep,
For men who have their will
Have gained a good they cannot keep,
And must go down the hill

Not questioning the seas and skies,
Not questioning the years;
For life itself has closed their eyes,
And life has stopped their ears.

But some, true emperors of desire,
True heirs to all regret,
Strangers and pilgrims, still enquire
For what they never get.

For what they know is not on earth
They seek until they find;
The children hopeful in their mirth,
The old but part resigned.

And though they cannot see love's face
They tread his former track;
They know him by his empty place,
They know him by their lack.

I seek the company of such,
I wear that worn attire;
For I am one who has had much,
But not the heart's desire.

Ruth Pitter

THE SEEKERS

Friends and loves we have none, nor wealth nor blest abode,
But the hope of the City of God at the other end of the road.

Not for us are content, and quiet, and peace of mind,
For we are seeking a city that we shall never find.

There is no solace on earth for us—for such as we—
Who search for a hidden city that we shall never see.

Only the road and the dawn, the sun, the wind, and the rain,
And the watch fire under stars, and sleep, and the road again.

We seek the City of God, and the haunt where beauty dwells,
And we find the noisy mart and the sound of burial bells.

Never the golden city, where the radiant people meet,
But the dolorous town where mourners are going about the
   street.

We travel the dusty road till the light of the day is dim,
And sunset shows us spires away on the world's rim.

We travel from dawn to dusk, till the day is past and by,
Seeking the Holy City beyond the rim of the sky.

Friends and loves we have none, nor wealth nor blest abode,
But the hope of the City of God at the other end of the road.

John Masefield

THE GUARDIANS

The guardians said: 'Wait for him if you like.
Often he comes when called, this time he may.
You will know it when the hawk, ruffling to strike,
Glimpses his white coat, and forbears to slay.
If it be in his mind, he will
Come at twilight to the dark pool.'

I said, 'Since childhood I have watched for him,
Burying this head so heavy with so much
Confusion, in my hands, while the world, dim
With many twilights, spun toward his touch.
Through a child's fingers then the time of love
Flowered in his eyes, and became alive.

'Sorrow walks after love: our childhood dies.
My twenty years of fighting came to this:
The brown eyes of my love looked in my eyes,
Beautiful in farewell, at our last kiss.
Her eyes like his eyes dealt so deep a wound,
Until he touch it, it will itch in wind.'

The guardians with stone flesh and faces of
Crumpled and heavy lines, stared at me.
With neither pity nor the fear of love,
Each stony hand clenched on a stony knee.
Grinding, like a crushed stone, each voice said, 'Let
Time pass. Pray you are not too late.'

Dom Moraes

THE FIDDLE AND THE BOW

This is what the fiddle said to the bow:
'No! oh no!
You should have warned me before the touch
of music, that it hurt too much.

You should have warned me, you should have told me,
before you let the music hold me,
how this poor wood were fain to melt
into the beauty it has felt.

How for one breathless note it trembles
almost on the edge of flame, then tumbles,
wounded with the sense of mortal things,
down, down, down, down with broken wings.

It was not right to wound and wake me.
Give me my silence back, or take me
wholly, and never let me go.'
That is what the fiddle said to the bow.

But the bow said 'How shall I guess
what bids me answer, 'Yes! oh yes!'
Since a greater thing than we are thus
for its blind purpose uses us?

We did not choose our way of making,
not sleeping ours to choose, nor waking,
not ours the starry strokes of sound
to choose or fly, though ours the wound.

Though dead wood cry, 'How shall I dare it?'
and wood reply, 'I cannot bear it,'
Yet his alone to choose, whose fingers
take the dead wood, and make his singers.

And if of dust he shapes this brittle
lift of the wings, this song's one petal
that shines and dies, is it not just
to suffer for song, oh, singing dust?

His was the choice, and if he wake us
out of the wood, but will not slake us,
thus stirred with the stars, at least we know
what pain the stars have,' says the bow.

                                        Humbert Wolfe

IN CHURCH

Often I try
To analyse the quality
Of its silence. Is this where God hides
From my searching? I have stopped to listen,
After the few people have gone,

To the air recomposing itself
For vigil. It has waited like this
Since the stones grouped themselves about it.
These are the hard ribs
Of a body that our prayers have failed
To animate. Shadows advance
From their corners to take possession
Of places the light held
For an hour. The bats resume
Their business. The uneasiness of the pews
Ceases. There is no other sound
In the darkness but the sound of a man
Breathing, testing his faith
On emptiness, nailing his questions
One by one to an untenanted cross.

R. S. Thomas

PRAYER TO ST. LUCY

At this our solstice of history,
Santa Lucia, pray for me—
You, whose too bright, offending eyes
Like leonids fell from your face of skies;
Since I must do my difficult work,
Sixty per cent, at least, in the dark,
Ascended virgin make petition
I am not quite blinded by erudition,
Lest the black pride of intellect
My senses, or my heart, infect.
These are the years where, still in vain,
We scan the unlimited heavens of pain,
Searching for an absconded God
(Yet under judgment, under His rod);
But may your wintry feast disclose
The first snowdrop, the Christmas rose—
Those white-clothed virgins of the earth,
The naked maiden, the plant of birth—
And faith is the substance of things not seen,

Under the snows of time, the green
Shoots of eternity; so, eyes being gone,
Still, still in the heart, the sun shines on.

John Heath-Stubbs

THE DIFFICULT LAND

This is a difficult land. Here things miscarry
Whether we care, or do not care enough.
The grain may pine, the harlot weed grow haughty,
Sun, rain, and frost alike conspire against us:
You'd think there was malice in the very air.
And the spring floods and summer droughts: our fields
Mile after mile of soft and useless dust.
On dull delusive days presaging rain
We yoke the oxen, go out harrowing,
Walk in the middle of an ochre cloud,
Dust rising before us and falling again behind us,
Slowly and gently settling where it lay.

These days the earth itself looks sad and senseless.
And when next day the sun mounts hot and lusty
We shake our fists and kick the ground in anger.
We have strange dreams: as that, in the early morning
We stand and watch the silver drift of stars
Turn suddenly to a flock of black-birds flying.
And once in a lifetime men from over the border,
In early summer, the season of fresh campaigns,
Come trampling down the corn, and kill our cattle.
These things we know and by good luck or guidance
Either frustrate or, if we must, endure.
We are a people; race and speech support us,
Ancestral rite and custom, roof and tree,
Our songs that tell of our triumphs and disasters
(Fleeting alike), continuance of fold and hearth,
Our names and callings, work and rest and sleep,
And something that, defeated, still endures—
These things sustain us. Yet there are times

When name, identity, and our very hands,
Senselessly labouring, grow most hateful to us,
And we would gladly rid us of these burdens,
Enter our darkness through the doors of wheat
And the light veil of grass (leaving behind
Name, body, country, speech, vocation, faith)
And gather into the secrecy of the earth
Furrowed by broken ploughs lost deep in time.
We have such hours, but are drawn back again
By faces of goodness, faithful masks of sorrow,
Honesty, kindness, courage, fidelity,
The love that lasts a life's time. And the fields,
Homestead and stall and barn, springtime and autumn.
(For we can love even the wandering seasons
In their inhuman circuit.) And the dead
Who lodge in us so strangely, unremembered,
Yet in their place. For how can we reject
The long last look on the ever-dying face
Turned backward from the other side of time?
And how offend the dead and shame the living
By these despairs? And how refrain from love?
This is a difficult country, and our home.

Edwin Muir

THE LABOURER

There he goes, tacking against the fields'
Uneasy tides. What have the centuries done
To change him? The same garments, frayed with light
Or seamed with rain, cling to the wind-scoured bones
And shame him in the eyes of the spruce birds.
Once it was ignorance, then need, but now
Habit that drapes him on a bush of cloud
For life to mock at, while the noisy surf
Of people dins far off at the world's rim.
He has been here since life began, a vague
Movement among the roots of the young grass.
Bend down and peer beneath the twigs of hair,

And look into the hard eyes, flecked with care;
What do you see? Notice the twitching hands,
Veined like a leaf, and tough bark of the limbs,
Wrinkled and gnarled, and tell me what you think.
A wild tree still, whose seasons are not yours,
The slow heart beating to the hidden pulse,
Of the strong sap, the feet firm in the soil?
No, no, a man like you, but blind with tears
Of sweat to the bright star that draws you on.

R. S. Thomas

Death is a clean bold word and has no second meaning.
Death means an end. By sight, touch, temperature we know.
Do not insult this strong word with a weak evasion
And say, 'He has gone on'—'He passed away'—'He sleeps.'

Speak not of the body and its lively grace
As paltry things that never mattered after all,
Creative hands and giving hands, hands calloused and deformed
As being nothing now but broken tools.

If you believe the soul, denied the dear familiar flesh,
Finds other place to live, keep to your faith,
But grant the body it illumined your candid grief.

Or if you must believe that when the light went out
Of eyes you loved and they stared back and told you nothing,
For that was all that could be told forever,
Salute Death. He demands you shall attain

Your fullest strength of honesty and courage.
You shall not bear your sorrow's weight upon a crutch of
   words,
You will stand straight, nor say your lover, friend, your child
Has 'gone' as though he'd wandered off somewhere,
But speak with dignity and say, 'He died.'

Rebecca Richmond

PART XIII

FINAL PEACE

'. . . ALL GONE . . .'

'Age takes in pitiless hands
All one loves most away;
Peace, joy, simplicity
Where then their inward stay?'

Or so, at least they say.

'Marvel of noontide light,
Of gradual break of day;
Dreams, visions of the night
   Age withers all away.'

Yes, that is what they say.

'Wonder of winter snow,
Magic of wandering. moon,
The starry hosts of heaven—
Come seventy, all are gone.

'Unhappy when alone,
Nowhere at peace to be;
Drowned the old self-sown eager thoughts
Constantly stirring in thee!' . . .

Extraordinary!
That's what they say to me!

                Walter de la Mare

So just as a good mariner when he draws near to the harbour
lets down his sails, and enters it gently with slight headway on;
so we ought to let down the sails of our worldly pursuits, and
turn to God with all our understanding and heart, so that we

may come to that haven with all composure and with all peace. And our own nature gives us a good lesson in gentleness, in so far as there is in such a death no pain, nor any bitterness; but as a ripe apple lightly and without violence detaches itself from its bough, so our soul severs itself without suffering from the body where it has dwelt.

Dante

HIS WISH TO GOD

I would to God, that mine old age might have
Before my last, but here a living grave,
Some one poor alms-house, there to lie, or stir,
Ghost-like, as in my meaner sepulchre;
A little piggin, and a pipkin by,
To hold things fitting my necessity;
Which, rightly us'd, both in their time and place,
Might me excite to fore, and after-grace.
Thy cross, my *Christ*, fixed 'fore mine eyes should be.
Not to adore that, but to worship thee.
So here the remnant of my days I'd spend,
Reading thy bible, and my book; so end.

Robert Herrick

AN EPITAPH

O mortal folk, you may behold and see
How I lie here, sometime a mighty knight;
The end of joy and all prosperitee
  Is death at last, thorough his course and might:
  After the day there cometh the dark night,
    For though the daye be never so long,
    At last the bells ringeth to evensong.

Stephen Hawes

THE DYING CHRISTIAN TO HIS SOUL

I

Vital spark of heav'nly flame!
Quit, oh quit this mortal frame:
Trembling, hoping, ling'ring, flying,
Oh the pain, the bliss of dying!
Cease, fond Nature, cease thy strife,
And let me languish into life.

II

Hark! they whisper; Angels say,
Sister Spirit, come away.
What is this absorbs me quite?
Steals my senses, shuts my sight,
Drowns my spirits, draws my breath?
Tell me, my Soul, can this be Death?

III

The world recedes; it disappears!
Heav'n opens on my eyes! my ears
With sound seraphic ring:
Lend, lend your wings! I mount! I fly!
O Grave! where is thy Victory?
O Death! where is thy Sting?

Alexander Pope

I AM

I am: yet what I am none cares or knows,
My friends forsake me like a memory lost;
I am the self-consumer of my woes,
They rise and vanish in oblivious host,
Like shades of love and death's oblivion lost;
And yet I am, and live with shadows tost

Into the nothingness of scorn and noise,
Into the living sea of waking dreams,

Where there is neither sense of life nor joys
   But the vast shipwreck of my life's esteems;
And e'en the dearest—that I loved the best—
Are strange—nay, rather stranger than the rest.

I long for scenes where man has never trod,
   A place where woman never smiled or wept;
There to abide with my Creator, God,
   And sleep as I in childhood sweetly slept:
Untroubling and untroubled where I lie,
The grass below—above the vaulted sky.

John Clare   Written in Northampton Asylum

THE RECALL

I am the land of their fathers.
In me the virtue stays.
I will bring back my children,
After certain days.

Under their feet in the grasses
My clinging magic runs.
They shall return as strangers.
They shall remain as sons.

Over their heads in the branches
Of their new-bought, ancient trees,
I weave an incantation
And draw them to my knees.

Scent of smoke in the evening,
Smell of rain in the night—
The hours, the days and the seasons,
Order their souls aright,

Till I make plain the meaning
Of all my thousand years—
Till I fill their hearts with knowledge,
While I fill their eyes with tears.

Rudyard Kipling

FOR MY FUNERAL

O thou that from thy mansion
　　Through time and place to roam
Dost send abroad thy children,
　　And thou dost call them home.

That men and tribes and nations
　　And all thy hand hath made
May shelter them from sunshine
　　In thine eternal shade:

We now to peace and darkness
　　And earth and thee restore
Thy creature that thou madest
　　And wilt cast forth no more.

　　　　　　　　　　　　A. E. Housman

MARGARITAE SORORI

A late lark twitters from the quiet skies:
And from the west,
Where the sun, his day's work ended,
Lingers as in content,
There falls on the old, gray city
An influence luminous and serene,
A shining peace.

The smoke ascends
In a rosy-and-golden haze. The spires
Shine and are changed. In the valley
Shadows rise. The lark sings on. The sun,
Closing his benediction,
Sinks, and the darkening air
Thrills with a sense of the triumphing night—
Night with her train of stars
And her great gift of sleep.

So be my passing!
My task accomplish'd and the long day done,
My wages taken, and in my heart
Some late lark singing,
Let me be gather'd to the quiet west,
The sundown splendid and serene,
Death.

William Ernest Henley

DELIVERANCE

Through naked sticks, his winter bones,
 The dead wind blew the snow,
Man was the scaffold of disaster,
 The trembling net of woe.

His starving veins were frozen strings,
 They rigged his skeleton,
The hailstones cracked his tattered skins
 But could not drive him on.

His howling eyeballs could not know,
 Searching the dreadful night,
Which gleam was star, or scimitar,
 Or which the beacon light.

He thought: 'I am the cage of pain,
 A trap for every sorrow,
Yet one day, as I comb this storm,
 Shall I not catch the swallow?'

The black wind drops, at last the sun
 With green dust beats the air,
His hands and skull with blossoms fill,
 His crown sprouts grassy hair.

His sick veins now do spring alive,
 Leaves run along each bone,

And in his hollow eyes the birds
   Sing out for him alone.

Trimmed like a lamp and warm with love
   He shouts his noisy blood,
No sound recalls that age of grief,
   No memory doubts this Good.

Laurie Lee

BELLS FOR WILLIAM WORDSWORTH

Today they brought me a message: Wordsworth was dead.
'My God,' I said. 'My God. I can hardly believe it.'
'Just as you like,' they answered. 'Take it or leave it,
He has sunk into April as into the depths of a lake,
Leaving his eyes ajar in the house of his head.'
'Are you sure,' I said, 'that you haven't made a mistake?'

'Oh no,' they said, 'not a hope. We knew him too well,
A gloomy considering bloke with the nose of a preacher:
A poet, in fact, with a charming affection for Nature:
Milkmaids (you know) and the shadows of clouds on the land.
His work is carefully studied in colleges still.
We shall not forget nor forgo it, while colleges stand.'

And I said, 'I grant you that Wordsworth lies chilly in Grasmere
And his bones are absolved and dissolved in the tears of the rain.
I grant he is one with the plant and the fossil again,
His flesh has gone back into soil and his eyes into stones
And the roots and shoots of a new life push each year
Through the sad rotten fragments of his bones.

'But although each Spring brings a newer death to those bones,
I have seen him risen again with the crocus in Spring.
I have turned my ear to the wind, I have heard him speaking.
I shrank from the bony sorrow in his face.
Yet still I hear those pedagogic tones
Droning away the snow, our old disgrace.'

Dom Moraes

243

O Maker of the starry world,
Who, resting on thy everlasting throne,
Turnst heaven like a spindle,
And hast the stars brought under law,
So that the moon, now shining at the full,
Straight in the pathway of her brother's flame,
Blots out the lesser stars :
Now with her crescent dim
Draws near the sun and loses all her light :
And Hesperus, in the first hour of eve,
Awakens the cold welling of the stars,
And then as Lucifer
Grows pallid in the rising of the sun.
It is thy power tempers the changing year
So that the leaves the North Wind swept away
The West Wind brings again.
Arcturus watched the sowing of the seed
That Sirius parches in the standing grain.
Naught is there that escapes the ancient law,
Or leaves the work of its appointed ward.
Thou guidest all things to their certain goal,
All but the ways of men :
Keep them in check thou wilt not.
O Ruler of the world, Thou has spat them out.
Why should the noxious consequence of sin
Take hold upon the sinless?
The pervert sits enthroned,
And ruffians set their heel on the neck of saints.
The just man bears the guilt of the unjust.
No perjury,
No fraud tricked out with gaudy lies,
Can damage evil men :

And when they have a mind to use their power
They take delight in subjugating kings
That kept the world in awe.
O Thou, who e'er thou art,
Thou who dost bind all things in covenant,
Now, now look down on these unhappy lands.

We are not the vilest part of thy creation,
Great though it be—men tossed on bitter seas.
Ruin in the surging of wild rushing waters,
And thou that rulest heaven's immensity,
By that same covenant, steady the earth.

O Father, give the spirit power to climb
To the fountain of all light, and be purified.
Break through the mists of earth, the weight of the clod,
Shine forth in splendour, Thou that are calm weather,
And quiet resting place for faithful souls.
To see thee is the end and the beginning,
Thou carriest us, and Thou dost go before,
Thou art the journey, and the journey's end.

King Alfred's translation of Boethius

STORM

I have seen daylight turn cadaverous,
And on the earth the fixed defeated look,
The grim north light, as on the face of the dead
Reflected up from the wan-shining sea
Where they put forth utterly desolate;
Often have seen the hideous face of storm,
All in a moment changing balefully
Wholesome to fell, and homeliest to strange:
A yellow awe and a swift pestilence
Precipitating natural decays:
Till from the quarter of the awaited woe
Bows the whole landscape on a fleeting arc,
Heads, treetops, cornfields, all to leeward strain:
A billow heaped of the whole atmosphere,
A shriek that snatches at complete revenge,
Hurled like an airy war across the world,
Level the fields that shall not rise again,
And opening all the gates of upper flood,
Drown, blast and splinter, thunder above and below.
Have I not seen the sudden storm in the mind,

Conceived of anguish brooding wastefully,
Heaping the sullen forces baulked by life,
Harvesting blackness, gathering up rage,
Till at the last the spark, the seed of fire
Leaps from the cloud, and after comes the roar,
The deluge and the dire destructiveness,
And fields of tender thought are laid in mire.

But is there not the tempest-following calm,
The glitter, and the charm of a chilled air,
Songs poured while draggled plumes are fanned to dry,
And many buds' dun mantles beaten off,
While beauty new and naked opens and shines,
For every broken flower a score of heirs?
Does not the earth drink freshness audibly,
And all surviving things wax great and blow,
And with his strength renewed, the following sun
Make haste to wither the fallen out of sight,
And since they are dead to hurry them to dust?

Truly there is a tempest-following calm;
But if there be one of the mind I know not,
For I have never seen it. Her day is dim:
Her fairest day is one without alarms;
Cold was her dawn, colder shall be her night.
Her isle is circled by the hopeless sea
Which she may pass only by way of death:
Tempest or leaden calm, the grim north light
Is on her countenance reflected up,
And utterly bereaved of the soul's sun,
If such there be, sullen she labours on,
Still hoping faintly to be staunch enough
To weather the remaining tale of storms,
To make her landfall in the unknown place
Where the miraculous freshness falls like dew,
And on her face the sun incredible,
Long-fabled, legendary, and unhoped-for, shines.

Ruth Pitter

IN THE OPEN

Move into the clear.
Keep still, take your stand
Out in the place of fear
On the bare sand;

Where you have never been,
Where the small heart is chilled;
Where a small thing is seen,
And can be killed.

Under the open day,
So weak and so appalled,
Look up and try to say,
Here I am, for you called.

You must haunt the thin cover
By that awful place,
Till you can get it over
And look up into that face.

Ruth Pitter

O God, beloved God, in pity send
That blessed rose among the thorns—an end:
Give a bruised spirit peace.

John Masefield

TO MARY—A DEDICATION

Forgive what I give you. Through nightmare and cinders,
The one can be trodden, the other ridden,
We must use what transport we can. Both crunching
Path and bucking dream can take me
Where I shall leave the path and dismount
From the mad-eyed beast and keep my appointment
In green improbable fields with you.

Louis MacNeice

IN TROUBLE AND SHAME

I look at the swaling sunset
And wish I could go also
Through the red doors beyond the black-purple bar.

I wish that I could go
Through the red doors where I could put off
My shame like shoes in the porch,
My pain like garments,
And leave my flesh discarded lying
Like luggage of some departed traveller
Gone one knows not whither.

Then I would turn round,
And seeing my cast-off body lying like lumber,
I would laugh with joy.

D. H. Lawrence

THE BRIDE

My love looks like a girl tonight,
But she is old.
The plaits that lie along her pillow
Are not gold,
But threaded with filigree silver,
And uncanny cold.

She looks like a young maiden, since her brow
Is smooth and fair;
Her cheeks are very smooth, her eyes are closed,
She sleeps a rare,
Still, winsome sleep, so still, and so composed.

Nay, but she sleeps like a bride, and dreams her dreams
Of perfect things.
She lies at last, the darling, in the shape of her dream,
And her dead mouth sings
By its shape, like thrushes in clear evenings.

D. H. Lawrence

CALL INTO DEATH

Since I lost you, my darling, the sky has come near,
And I am of it, the small sharp stars are quite near,
The white moon going among them like a white bird among
    snow-berries,
And the sound of her gently rustling in heaven like a bird I hear.

And I am willing to come to you now, my dear,
As a pigeon lets itself off from a cathedral dome
To be lost in the haze of the sky; I would like to come
And be lost out of sight with you, like a melting foam.

For I am tired, my dear, and if I could lift my feet,
My tenacious feet, from off the dome of the earth
To fall like a breath within the breathing wind
Where you are lost, what rest, my love, what rest!

                            D. H. Lawrence

TORCHBEARER

I saw your hands lying at peace
at last, and I thought of Helen's hands
that were not lovelier than these,
yet live in all men's minds.
And I thought 'beauty is not trapped
even in this delicate
dust, these hands, but was shaped
elsewhere inviolate.'
And I thought 'there is one mould
and these hands, in beauty set,
pass the torch, lit from of old,
to hands that are not yet.'
Therefore I do not bid farewell,
torchbearer! for you belong
now to the imperishable
foundation of song.

                            Humbert Wolfe

Naked, he sags across her cumbered knees,
Heavy and beautiful like the child she once
Aroused from sleep, to fall asleep on the next breath.

The passion is done,
But death has not yet stiffened him against her,
Nor chilled the stripling grace into a dogma.
For a timeless hour, imagined out of marble,
He come back to his mother, he is all
And only hers.

And it is she whom death has magnified
To bear the burden of his flesh—the arms
Excruciated no more, the gash wiped clean.
A divine, dazed compassion calms her features.
She holds all earth's dead sons upon her lap.

C. Day Lewis from Pietà

. . . Nothing is here for tears, nothing to wail
Or knock the breast, no weakness, no contempt,
Dispraise, or blame, nothing but well and fair,
And what may quiet us in a death so noble . . .

Milton from Samson Agonistes

When the Lord turned again the captivity of Zion, we were like them that dream.

Then was our mouth filled with laughter, and our tongue with singing; then said they among the heathen, The Lord hath done great things for them.

The Lord hath done great things for us; whereof we are glad.

Turn again our captivity, O Lord, as the streams in the south.

They that sow in tears shall reap in joy.

He that goeth forth and weepeth, bearing precious seed, shall doubtless come again with rejoicing, bringing his sheaves with him.

Psalm 126

Part XIV

PEACEFUL HEAVENS

THE SPECTACLE

Scan with calm bloodshot eyes the world around us,
Its broken stones, its sorrows! No voice could tell
The toll of the innocent crucified, weeping and wailing,
In this region of torment ineffable, flame and derision—
    What wonder if we believe no longer in Hell?

    And Heaven? That daybreak vision?
In the peace of our hearts we learn beyond shadow of doubting
That our dream of this vanished kingdom lies sleeping within
      us;
Its gates are the light we have seen in the hush of the morning,
When the shafts of the sunrise break in a myriad splendours;
Its shouts of joy are those of all earthly creatures,
Their primal and innocent language—the song of the birds:
Thrush in its rapture, ecstatic wren, and wood-dove tender,
Calling on us poor mortals to put our praise into words.

Passionate, sorrowful hearts, too—the wise, the true and the
      gentle;
Minds that outface all fear, defy despair, remain faithful,
Endure in silence, hope on, assured in their selfless courage,
Natural and sweet in a love no affliction or doubt could dispel.

If, as a glass reflecting its range, we have these for our guidance,
If, as our love creates beauty, we exult in that transient
      radiance,
This is the garden of paradise which in our folly
    We abandoned long ages gone.

Though, then, the wondrous divine were ev'n nebulae-distant,
The little we make of our all is our earthly heaven.
    Else we are called in a darkness,
Windowless, doorless, alone.

Walter de la Mare

THE DAY WITH A WHITE MARK

All day I have been tossed and whirled in a preposterous
    happiness:
Was it an elf in the blood? or a bird in the brain? or even part
Of the cloudily crested, fifty-league long, loud uplifted wave
Of a journeying angel's transit roaring over and through my
    heart?

My garden's spoiled, my holidays are cancelled, the omens
    harden;
The plann'd and unplann'd miseries deepen; the knots draw
    tight.
Reason kept telling me all day my mood was out of season.
It was, too. In the dark ahead the breakers only are white.

Yet I—I could have kissed the very scullery taps. The colour of
My day was like a peacock's chest. In at each sense there stole
Ripplings and dewy sprinkles of delight that with them drew
Fine threads of memory through the vibrant thickness of the
    soul.

As though there were transparent earths and luminous trees
    should grow there,
And shining roots worked visibly far down below one's feet,
So everything, the tick of the clock, the cock crowing in the
    yard
Probing my soul, woke diverse buried hearts of mine to beat,

Recalling either adolescent heights and the inaccessible
Longings and ice-sharp joys that shook my body and turned me
    pale,
Or humbler pleasures, chuckling as it were in the ear, mumbling
Of glee, as kindly animals talk in a children's tale.

Who knows if ever it will come again, now the day closes?
No-one can give me, or take away, that key. All depends
On the elf, the bird, or the angel. I doubt if the angel himself
Is free to choose when sudden heaven in man begins or ends.

C. S. Lewis

IN NO STRANGE LAND

O world invisible, we view thee,
  O world intangible, we touch thee,
O world unknowable, we know thee,
  Inapprehensible, we clutch thee!

Does the fish soar to find the ocean,
  The eagle plunge to find the air
That we ask of the stars in motion
  If they have rumour of thee there?

Not where the wheeling systems darken,
  And our benumbed conceiving soars!
The drift of pinions, would we harken,
  Beats at our own clay-shuttered doors.

The angels keep their ancient places;—
  Turn but a stone and start a wing!
'Tis ye, 'tis your estranged faces,
  That miss the many-splendoured thing.

And (when so sad thou canst not sadder)
  Cry, and upon thy so sore loss
Shall shine the traffic of Jacob's ladder
  Pitched between Heaven and Charing Cross.

Yea, in the night, my Soul, my daughter,
  Cry, clinging heaven by the hems:
And lo, Christ walking on the water,
  Not of Gennesaret, but Thames!

Francis Thompson

THE SUFFICIENT PLACE

See, all the silver roads wind in, lead in
To this still place like evening. See, they come
Like messengers bearing gifts to this little house,

And this great hill worn down to a patient mound,
And there tall trees whose motionless branches bear
An aeon's summer foliage, leaves so thick
They seem to have robbed a world of shade, and kept
No room for all these birds that line the boughs
With heavier riches, leaf and bird and leaf.
Within the doorway stand
Two figures, Man and Woman, simple and clear
As a child's first images. Their manners are
Such as were known before the earliest fashion
Taught the Heavens guile. The room inside is like
A thought that needed thus much space to write on,
This much, no more. Here's all sufficient. None
That comes complains, and all the world comes here,
Comes, and goes out again, and comes again.
This is the Pattern, these the Archetypes,
Sufficient, strong, and peaceful. All outside
From end to end of the world is tumult. Yet
These roads do not turn in here but writhe on
Round the wild earth for ever. If a man
Should chance to find this place three times in time
His eyes are changed and make a summer silence
Amid the tumult, seeing the roads wind in
To their still home, the house and the leaves and birds.

Edwin Muir

CARE IN HEAVEN

How many times they do come (if you will receive it),
So gay, with a light hand, and a brisk pinion
Cutting the blue air, that stands above London, even—
So, in a phrase of song,
In a half-hour's peace, lying like a moment of love
Upon our wounds, affect us;
Telling we are only a footstep from the garden,
From the golden world, from the shoemakers' holiday—
How near we were to finding our lost childhood.

So courteous they are. Then why should we refuse them
If tomorrow they come back in their formal livery,
Their panolpy of humiliation, to pummel
With fiery sword-hilts upon the heart's closed doors?
These are dark nuncios; they have the king's commission.
Let it be Michaelmas: the falling of the leaf,
The time of the blue daisy—when the chief of the heavenly
    birds
Strikes at the glistening snake, who falls
Like a wreath, like a wraith of smoke, among
Those hemlock-umbels, the autumn constellations.

John Heath-Stubbs

SHE ASKS FOR A NEW EARTH

Lord, when I find at last Thy Paradise,
Be it not all too bright for human eyes,
Lest I go sick for home through the high mirth—
For Thy new Heaven, Lord, give me new earth.

Give of Thy mansions, Lord, a house so small
Where they can come to me who were my all;
Let them run home to me just as of yore,
Glad to sit down with me and go out no more.

Give me a garden, Lord, and a low hill,
A field and a babbling brook that is not still;
Give me an orchard, Lord, in leaf and bloom,
And my birds to sing to me in a quiet gloom.

There shall no canker be in leaf and bud,
But glory on hill and sea and the green-wood,
There, there shall none grow old but all be new,
No moth nor rust shall fret nor thief break through.

Set Thou a mist upon Thy glorious sun,
Lest we should faint for night and be undone;
Give us the high clean wind and the wild rain,
Lest that we faint with thirst and go in pain.

Let there be Winter there and the joy of Spring,
Summer and Autumn and the harvesting;
Give us all things we loved on earth of old
Never to slip from out our fond arms' fold.

Give me a little house for my desire,
The man and the children to sit by my fire,
And friends crowding in, to our lit hearth—
For Thy new Heaven, Lord, give me new earth!

Katharine Tynan

THE HOUSE OF CHRISTMAS

To an open house in the evening,
Home shall men come,
To an older place than Eden,
And a taller town than Rome.
To the end of the way of the wandering star,
To the things that cannot be and that are,
To the place where God was homeless,
And all men are at home.

G. K. Chesterton

THE HOLY OF HOLIES

'Elder Father, though thine eyes
Shine with hoary mysteries,
Canst thou tell what in the heart
Of a cowslip blossom lies?'

'Smaller than all lives that be,
Secret as the deepest sea,
Stands a little house of seeds
Like an elfin's granary.'

'Speller of the stones and weeds
Skilled in Nature's crafts and creeds,
Tell me what is in the heart
Of the smallest of the seeds.'

'God Almighty, and with Him
Cherubim and Seraphim,
Filling all eternity.
Adonai Elohim!'

G. K. Chesterton

PRAYER TO GO TO PARADISE WITH THE ASSES

O God, when You send for me, let it be
Upon some festal day of dusty roads.
I wish as I did ever here-below
By any road that pleases me, to go
To Paradise, where stars shine all day long.
Taking my stick out on the great highway,
To my dear friends the asses I shall say:
I am Francis Jammes going to Paradise,
For there is no hell where the Lord God dwells.
Come with me, my sweet friends of azure skies
You poor, dear beasts who whisk off with your ears
Mosquitoes, peevish blows, and buzzing bees . . .

Let me appear before You with these beasts,
Whom I so love because they bow their head
Sweetly, and halting join their little feet
So gently that it makes you pity them.
Let me come followed by their million ears,
By those that carried paniers on their flanks,
And those that dragged the cars of acrobats,
Those that had battered cans upon their backs,
She-asses limping, full as leather-bottles,
And those too that they breech because of blue
And oozing wounds round which the stubborn flies
Gather in swarms. God, let me come to You
With all these asses into Paradise.

Let angels lead us where your rivers soothe
Their tufted banks, and cherries, tremble, smooth
As is the laughing flesh of tender maids.
And let me, where Your perfect peace pervades,
Be like Your asses, bending down above
The heavenly waters through eternity,
To mirror their sweet, humble poverty
In the clear waters of eternal love.

Francis Jammes

THE PASSIONATE MAN'S PILGRIMAGE

Give me my scallop-shell of quiet,
My staff of faith to walk upon,
My scrip of joy, immortal diet,
My bottle of salvation,
My gown of glory, hope's true gage,
And thus I'll take my pilgrimage.

Blood must be my body's balmer,
No other balm will there be given,
Whilst my soul like a white palmer
Travels to the land of heaven,
Over the silver mountains,
Where spring the nectar fountains;
And there I'll kiss
The bowl of bliss,
And drink my everlasting fill
On every milken hill.
My soul will be a-dry before,
But after it will thirst no more.

And by the happy blissful way
More peaceful pilgrims I shall see,
That have shook off their gowns of clay
And go apparelled fresh like me.
I'll bring them first

To slake their thirst,
And then to taste those nectar suckets,
At the clear wells
Where sweetness dwells,
Drawn up by saints in crystal buckets.

And when our bottles and all we
Are filled with immortality,
Then the holy paths we'll travel,
Strewed with rubies thick as gravel,
Ceilings of diamonds, sapphire floors,
High walls of coral and pearl bowers.

From thence to heaven's bribeless hall
Where no corrupted voices brawl,
No conscience molten into gold,
Nor forged accusers bought and sold,
No cause deferred, nor vain-spent journey,
For there Christ is the King's Attorney,
Who pleads for all without degrees,
And he hath angels, but no fees.

When the grand twelve million jury
Of our sins and direful fury
'Gainst our souls black verdicts give,
Christ pleads his death, and then we live.
Be thou my speaker, taintless pleader,
Unblotted lawyer, true proceeder;
Thou movest salvation even for alms,
Not with a bribed lawyer's palms.

And this is my eternal plea
To him that made heaven, earth, and sea:
Seeing my flesh must die so soon,
And want a head to dine next noon,
Just at the stroke when my veins start and spread,
Set on my soul an everlasting head,
Then am I ready, like a palmer fit,
To treat those blest paths which before I writ.

Sir Walter Raleigh

PEACE

I sought for Peace, but could not find;
   I sought it in the city,
But they were of another mind,
   The more's the pity!

I sought for Peace of country swain,
   But yet I could not find;
So I, returning home again,
   Left Peace behind.

Sweet Peace, where dost thou dwell? said I.
   Methought a voice was given:
'Peace dwelt not here, long since did fly
   To God in heaven.'

Thought I, this echo is but vain,
   To folly 'tis of kin;
Anon I heard it tell me plain,
   'Twas killed by sin.

Then I believed the former voice,
   And rested well content,
Laid down and slept, rose, did rejoice,
   And then to heaven went.
There I enquired for Peace, and found it true,
An heavenly plant it was, and sweetly grew.

Samuel Speed

THE NEW GHOST

'And he casting away his garment rose and came to Jesus.'

And he cast it down, down, on the green grass,
Over the young crocuses, where the dew was—
He cast the garment of his flesh that was full of death,
And like a sword his spirit showed out of the cold sheath.

262

He went a pace or two, he went to meet his Lord,
And, as I said, his spirit looked like a clean sword,
And seeing him the naked trees began shivering,
And all the birds cried aloud as it were late spring.

And the Lord came on, He came down, and saw
That a soul was waiting there for Him, one without flaw,
And they embraced in the churchyard where the robins play,
And the daffodils hang their heads, as they burn away.

The Lord held his head fast, and you could see
That He kissed the unsheathed ghost that was gone free—
As a hot sun, on a March day, kisses the cold ground;
And the spirit answered, for he knew well that his peace was
   found.

The spirit trembled, and sprang up at the Lord's word—
As on a wild, April day, spring up a small bird—
So the ghost's feet lifting him up, he kissed the Lord's cheek,
And for the greatness of their love neither of them could speak.

But the Lord went then, to show him the way,
Over the young crocuses, under the green may
That was not quite in flower yet—to a far-distant land;
And the ghost followed, like a naked cloud holding the sun's
   hand.

Fredegond Shove

THE BLESSED RECEIVED IN PARADISE

(After the painting by Giovanni di Paolo)

Here in this dark and radiant glade, wearing the sun's
familiar robes, they greet mortality with an immortal grace.
To the diviner music of the spheres they move, and weave,
with more than human tenderness, anemone and wild
ranunculus, for crowns that do not fade. The animals of childhood

wander fearlessly beside them among the moving trees,
and find no need for speech; for all here are dumb
with paradise, where to be silent is to be understood.

They walk in real freedom here, on pointed feet
that tread the miracle of one green spring
remembered perfectly. The drowned sailor feels the wind
breathe like the deep's gentle current in his hair,
and lovers wonder at the fragrance of the air, this sweet
remembrance of a bitter parting in the breathless earth.
At last, the lost companions embrace, the young boy
smiles at his mother's kiss again, and at his father's face.

James Kirkup

THE NEW JERUSALEM

Hierusalem, my happy home,
   When shall I come to thee?
When shall my sorrows have an end,
   Thy joys when shall I see?

O happy harbour of the Saints!
   O sweet and pleasant soil!
In thee no sorrow may be found,
   No grief, no care, no toil.

There lust and lucre cannot dwell,
   There envy bears no sway;
There is no hunger, heat, nor cold,
   But pleasure every way.

Thy walls are made of precious stones,
   Thy bulwarks diamonds square;
Thy gates are of right orient pearl,
   Exceeding rich and rare.

Thy turrets and thy pinnacles
   With carbuncles do shine;
Thy very streets are paved with gold,
   Surpassing clear and fine.

Ah, my sweet home, Hierusalem,
   Would God I were in thee!
Would God my woes were at an end,
   Thy joys that I might see!

Thy gardens and thy gallant walks
   Continually are green;
There grow such sweet and pleasant flowers
   As nowhere else are seen.

Quite through the streets, with silver sound,
   The flood of Life doth flow;
Upon whose banks on every side
   The wood of Life doth grow.

There trees for evermore bear fruit,
   And evermore do spring;
There evermore the angels sit,
   And evermore do sing.

Our Lady sings *Magnificat*
   With tones surpassing sweet;
And all the virgins bear their part,
   Sitting about her feet.

Hierusalem, my happy home,
   Would God I were in thee!
Would God my woes were at an end,
   Thy joys that I might see!

Song of Mary the Mother of Christ (*London: E. Allde*)

The day now approaching when she was to depart this life,—which day Thou knowest but we not,—it came to pass, thyself, as I believe, by thy secret ways so ordering it, that she and I stood alone, leaning in a certain window which looked on the garden of the house wherein we lodged at Ostia; for there before our voyage we were resting in quiet from the fatigues of a long journey. Discoursing then together alone very sweetly, and forgetful of the past, and reaching forth unto those things which are before, we were enquiring between ourselves in the presence of the truth, which Thou art, of what sort the eternal life of the saints may be, which eye hath not seen, nor ear heard, nor hath it entered into the heart of man. And all the while did our hearts within us gasp after the heavenly strains of thy fountain, the well of Life, which is in Thee, that being sprinkled thence according to our measure, we might in some sort meditate on so high a mystery.

And as our talk was leading us thither where we would be, so that no delight of the senses whatsoever, in any brightness possible to them, seemed in respect of the joy of that life worthy of mention, far less of comparison, we upraising ourselves with intenser desire unto that Self-same, went on to explore in turn all things material, even the very heaven, whence sun and moon and stars give light upon the earth : and thus ascending by meditation and speech and admiration of thy works, we were drawing yet nearer, and had come to our own minds, and left them behind, that we might arrive at the country of unfailing plenty, where Thou feedest thy people for ever in pastures of truth; there where life is the WISDOM by which all those thy works are made, that have been or that shall be; Wisdom uncreate, the same now as it ever was, and the same to be for evermore. Nay rather to have been and hereafter to be cannot be spoken of it, but only to be, since it is eternal. . . . Of that heavenly Wisdom as then we talked and hunger'd after it, lo, with the whole effort of our heart we apprehended somewhat thereof : and we sighed, and abandoning on that far shore those firstfruits of the spirit, we fell back to the sound of our own voices, and the determinate words of human discourse. . . .

And we began to say, If to any the tumult of the flesh were

hushed; hushed the images of earth, of waters and of air; hushed also the poles of heaven; yea, were the very soul to be hushed to herself, and by not thinking on self to surmount self; hushed all dreams and imaginary revelations, every tongue and every sign; if all transitory things were hushed utterly,— for to him that heareth they do all speak, saying 'we made not ourselves, but He made us, who abideth for ever'—; if, when their speech had gone out they should suddenly hold their peace, and to the ear which they had aroused to their Maker, He himself should speak, alone, not by them, but by himself, so that we should hear his word, not through any tongue of flesh, nor Angel's voice, nor echo of thunder, nor in the dark riddle of a similitude, but might hear indeed Him, whom in these things we love, himself without these,—as we but now with effort and in swift thought touched on that eternal Wisdom, which abideth over all—; could this be continued, and all disturbing visions of whatever else be withdrawn, and this one ravish and absorb, and wrap up its beholder amid these inward joys, so that life might ever be like that one moment of understanding, which but now we sighed after; were not this ENTER THOU INTO THE JOY OF THY LORD?

The Ecstasy of S. Augustin and S. Monica

The peace of the celestial city is the perfectly ordered and harmonious enjoyment of God and of one another in God. The peace of all things is the tranquillity of order.

St. Augustine from The City of God

The wilderness and the solitary place shall be glad for them; and the desert shall rejoice, and blossom as the rose.

It shall blossom abundantly, and rejoice even with joy and singing: the glory of Lebanon shall be given unto it, the excellency of Carmel and Sharon, they shall see the glory of the Lord, and the excellency of our God.

Strengthen ye the weak hands, and confirm the feeble knees.

Say to them that are of a fearful heart, Be strong, fear not: behold, your God will come with vengeance, even God with a recompence; he will come and save you.

Then the eyes of the blind shall be opened, and the ears of the deaf shall be unstopped.

Then shall the lame man leap as an hart, and the tongue of the dumb sing: for in the wilderness shall waters break out, and streams in the desert.

And the parched ground shall become a pool, and the thirsty land springs of water: in the habitation of dragons, where each lay, shall be grass with reeds and rushes.

And an highway shall be there, and a way, and it shall be called The way of holiness; the unclean shall not pass over it; but it shall be for those: the wayfaring men, though fools, shall not err therein.

No lion shall be there, nor any ravenous beast shall go up thereon, it shall not be found there; but the redeemed shall walk there.

And the ransomed of the Lord shall return, and come to Zion with songs and everlasting joy upon their heads: they shall obtain joy and gladness, and sorrow and sighing shall flee away.

Isaiah (Chapter 35)

PART XV

THE PEACE OF GOD

THE PEACE OF GOD

Lord put thou my tears in thy sight and my hearty prayer fully come into heaven to thee.

Lead me forth into the path of light, into the dearest country of men living, set me in the siker rest-folds of thy flocks, which art a good shepherd, which again-seekest and again-leadest things lost, defendest and savest things found, nourishest and makest whole sick things.

And thou art merciful Lord, which confoundest not men hoping in thee, forsakest not men again-seeking thee, puttest not men away, again-turning to thee, but receivest in full-out joying and praising, and grantest to reign everlastingly in bliss together with thy saints and with thy chosen. For one Godhead, glory, virtue, honour, empire and power be to thee with the Father everlasting and Holy Ghost, into worlds of worlds. Amen.

From Pseudo-Augustine   Treatise to an earl

Thus saw I that God is our very Peace, and He is our sure Keeper when we are ourselves in unpeace, and He continually worketh to bring us into endless peace.

Full preciously our Lord keepeth us when it seemeth to us that we are near forsaken and cast away for our sin and because we have deserved it. And because of meekness that we get hereby, we are raised well-high in God's sight by His grace, with so great contrition, and also compassion, and true longing to God. Then they be suddenly delivered from sin and from pain, and taken up to bliss, and made even high saints.

By contrition we are made clean, by compassion we are made ready, and by true longing toward God we are made worthy. These are three means, as I understand, whereby that all souls come to heaven: that is to say, that have been sinners in earth and shall be saved: for by these three medicines it behoveth

that every soul be healed. Though the soul be healed, his
wounds are seen afore God,—not as wounds but as worships.
And so on the contrary-wise, as we be punished here with
sorrow and penance, we shall be rewarded in heaven by the
courteous love of our Lord God Almighty, who willeth that
none that come there lose his travail in any degree. For he
(be)holdeth sin as sorrow and pain to His lovers, to whom He
assigneth no blame, for love. The meed that we shall receive
shall be little, but it shall be high, glorious, and worshipful. And
so shall shame be turned to worship and more joy.

But our courteous Lord willeth not that His servants despair,
for often nor for grievous falling: for our falling hindereth not
him to love us. Peace and love are ever in us, being and work-
ing; but we be not always in peace and in love. But he willeth
that we take heed thus that He is Ground of all our whole life
in love; and furthermore that He is our everlasting Keeper and
mightily defendeth us against our enemies.

Dame Julian of Norwich

Humility and patience in adversity more please me, my son,
    than much comfort and devotion in prosperity.
And why should a little thing spoken against thee make thee
    sad?
    had it been greater, thou shouldst not have been
    disturbed.
But now let it pass: 'tis nothing strange; it hath happed before;
    and if thou live longer, it will happen again.
Thou art manly enough while there is nought to oppose thee:
    thou canst give good counsel, and hast encouraged others
    with words:
But when suddenly the trouble cometh to thine own door,
    thou lackest to thyself both in courage and counsel.
Consider thy great weakness, which thou discoverest often in
    trifling concerns:
    and yet it is all for thy good, when these or such like things
    befal thee.
Put the matter as well as thou canst out of thy mind;
    and if the tribulation hath touched thee, let it not cast thee
    down nor entangle thee.

Bear it patiently, if gladly thou canst not:
  or even if thou resent this saying and feel indignation, yet
    govern thyself;
  nor suffer an unchastened word to escape thee, whereby the
    little ones may stumble.
The storm that hath arisen will quickly subside:
  and thy hidden pain will be soothed by returning grace.
I still Am, saith the Lord, ready to aid thee and console thee
    more than ever, .
  if thou but trust me, and beseech thee with all thy heart.
Be more tranquil in mind, and brace thyself to better fortitude:
  All is not lost, even though again and again thou feel thyself
    broken or well-nigh spent.

Thomas à Kempis

Grant me thy grace, most merciful Jesus, that it may be with
me, and may labour with me, and continue with me to the
end. . . .
Let Thy will be mine, and let my will always follow Thine,
and agree perfectly therewith. . . .
Grant that I may rest in Thee above all things that can be
desired, and that my heart may be at peace in Thee.
Thou art the true peace of the heart, Thou art its only rest;
out of Thee all things are irksome and restless.
In this very peace which is in Thee, the one Supreme Eternal
Good, I will sleep and take my rest.

Thomas à Kempis

There lives no man on earth who may always have rest and
peace without troubles and crosses, with whom things go
always according to his will. There is always something to be
suffered here, consider it as you will. Seek only that true peace
of the heart, which none can take away from you, that you
may overcome all adversity; the peace that breaks through all
adversities and crosses, all oppression, suffering, misery, humili-
ation, and what more there may be of the like, so that a man
may be joyful and patient therein. Now if a man were lovingly
to give his whole diligence and might thereto, he could very

soon come to know that true eternal peace which is God Himself, as far as it is possible to a creature; insomuch that his heart would remain ever unmoved among all things.

Theologia Germanica

Give peace, that is, continue and preserve it; give peace, that is, give us hearts worthy of it, and thankful for it. In our time, that is, all our time: for there is more besides a fair morning required to make a fair day.

Thomas Fuller

It is nature which teacheth a wise man in fear to hide himself, but grace and faith doth teach him where. Fools care not where they hide their heads. . . . But because we are in danger like chased birds, like doves that seek and cannot see the resting holes that are right before them, therefore our Saviour giveth his disciples these encouragements beforehand, that fear might never so amaze them, but that always they might remember, that whatsoever evils at any time did beset them, to him they should still repair, for comfort, counsel, and succour.

Hooker

Our wills are quiescent in the nature of love; here love is fate; and in this blessed being all our wills are held in the divine will, where all are made into one will; and his will is our peace.

Dante

All things in motion desire to make known their own proper movement, and this is an aspiration after the Divine Peace of the whole, which, unfalling, preserves all things from falling, and, unmoved, guards the idiosyncracy and life of all moving things, so that the things moved, being at peace among themselves, perform their own proper functions.

Dionysius the Areopagite

To thee, O God, we turn for peace . . . but grant us too the blessed assurance that nothing shall deprive us of that peace, neither ourselves, nor our foolish, earthly desires, nor my wild longings, nor the anxious craving of my heart.

Kierkegaard

THE UNIVERSAL PRAYER

Father of All! in ev'ry Age,
  In ev'ry Clime ador'd,
By Saint, by Savage, and by Sage,
  Jehoval, Jove, or Lord!

Thou Great First Cause, least understood:
  Who all my Sense confin'd
To know but this, that Thou art Good,
  And that myself am blind;

Yet gave me, in this dark Estate,
  To see the Good from Ill;
And binding Nature fast in Fate,
  Left free the Human Will.

What Conscience dictates to be done,
  Or warns me not to do,
This, teach me more than Hell to shun,
  That, more than Heav'n pursue.

What Blessings thy free Bounty gives,
  Let me not cast away;
For God is pay'd when Man receives,
  T'enjoy is to obey.

Yet not to Earth's contracted Span
    Thy Goodness let me bound,
Or think Thee Lord alone of Man,
    When thousand Worlds are round:

Let not this weak, unknowing hand
    Presume thy bolts to throw,
And deal damnation round the land,
    On each I judge thy Foe.

If I am right, thy grace impart,
    Still in the right to stay;
If I am wrong, oh teach my heart
    To find that better way.

Save me alike from foolish Pride,
    Or impious Discontent,
At aught thy Wisdom has deny'd,
    Or aught thy Goodness lent.

Teach me to feel another's Woe,
    To hide the Fault I see;
That Mercy I to others show,
    That Mercy show to me.

Mean tho' I am, not wholly so,
    Since quick'ned by thy Breath;
Oh lead me wheresoe'r I go,
    Thro' this day's Life or Death.

This day, be Bread and Peace my Lot:
    All else beneath the Sun,
Thou know'st if best bestow'd or not;
    And let Thy Will be done.

To thee, whose Temple is all Space,
    Whose Altar Earth, Sea, Skies,
One chorus let all Being raise,
    All Nature's Incense rise!

Alexander Pope

Thou art the sky and thou art the nest as well.

O thou beautiful, there in the nest it is thy love that encloses the soul with colours and sounds and odours.

There comes the morning with the golden basket in her right hand bearing the wreath of beauty, silently to crown the earth.

And there comes the evening over the lonely meadows deserted by herds, through trackless paths, carrying cool draughts of peace in her golden pitcher from the western ocean of rest.

But there, where spreads the infinite sky for the soul to take her flight in, reigns the stainless white radiance. There is no day nor night, nor form nor colour, and never, never a word.

Rabindranath Tagore. Number 67 from Gitanjali

From early childhood, even as hath been said,
From his sixth year he had been sent abroad
In summer to tend herbs: such was his task
Thenceforward till the later day of youth.
Oh then what soul was his, when, on the tops
Of the high mountains, he beheld the sun
Rise up and bathe the world in light! He look'd—
Ocean and earth, the solid frame of earth
And ocean's liquid mass beneath him lay
In gladness and deep joy. The clouds were touch'd,
And in their silent faces did he read
Unutterable love. Sound needed none,
Nor any voice of joy; his spirit drank
The spectacle; sensation, soul, and form
All melted into him; they swallow'd up
His animal being; in them did he live,
And by them did he live: they were his life.
In such access of mind, in such high hour
Of visitation from the living God,
Thought was not; in enjoyment it expired.
No thanks he breathed, he proffer'd no request;
Rapt into still communion that transcends
The imperfect offices of prayer and praise,
His mind was a thanksgiving to the Power
That made him; it was blessedness and love!

William Wordsworth

The sun, the moon, the stars, the seas, the hills and the plains—
Are not these, O Soul, the Vision of Him who reigns?

Is not the Vision He? tho' He be not that which He seems?
Dreams are true while they last, and do we not live in dreams?

Earth, these solid stars, this weight of body and limb,
Are they not sign and symbol of thy division from Him?

Dark is the world to thee: thyself art the reason why;
For is He not all but that which has power to feel 'I am I'?

Glory about thee, without thee; and thou fulfillest thy doom
Making Him broken gleams, and a stifled splendour and gloom.

Speak to Him thou for He hears, and Spirit with spirit can
    meet—
Closer is He than breathing, and nearer than hands and feet.

God is law, say the wise; O Soul, and let us rejoice,
For if He thunder by law the thunder is yet His voice.

Law is God, say some: no God at all, says the fool;
For all we have power to see is a straight staff bent in a pool;

And the ear of man cannot hear, and the eye of man cannot see;
But if we could see and hear, this Vision—were it not He?

Lord Tennyson

A NUN TAKES THE VEIL

I have desired to go
    Where springs not fail,
To fields where flies no sharp and sided hail
    And a few lilies grow.

And I have asked to be
    Where no storms come,
Where the green swell is in the heavens dumb,
    And out of the swing of the sea.

Gerard Manley Hopkins

THE HABIT OF PERFECTION

Elected Silence, sing to me
And beat upon my whorlèd ear,
Pipe me to pastures still and be
The music that I care to hear.

Shape nothing, lips; be lovely-dumb:
It is the shut, the curfew sent
From there where all surrenders come
Which only makes you eloquent.

Be shellèd, eyes, with double dark
And find the uncreated light:
This ruck and reel which you remark
Coils, keeps, and teases simple sight.

Palate, the hutch of tasty lust,
Desire not to be rinsed with wine:
The can must be so sweet, the crust
So fresh that come in fasts divine!

Nostrils, your careless breath that spend
Upon the stir and keep of pride,
What relish shall the censers send
Along the sanctuary side!

O feel-of-primrose hands, O feet
That want the yield of plushy sward,
But you shall walk the golden street
And you unhouse and house the Lord.

And, Poverty, be thou the bride
And now the marriage feast begun,
And lily-coloured clothes provide
Your spouse not laboured-at nor spun.

Gerard Manley Hopkins

LAMENT FOR ONE'S SELF

I know best what moan to make
Over my own dead;
Grieving aloud for my own sake,
Muttering at my grave's head.

Did you get what you wanted,
Fine child as you were?
I was harried and hunted
Till I took refuge here.

Did you see the fine sights
With your good clear eyes?
Foul sights and strange delights
Till blear age hid the skies.

My strong teeth that were so white
All went to decay;
My muscles and my clear sight
Wasted away.

Did you find the true heart
For whom you were born?
Never, for cold lust did part
Us in this place forlorn.

It is either that we are all mad,
Or my heart was born blind,
For every kind of love went bad
Between me and my kind.

Did you see nothing that could seem
Perfect, as life should be?
Yes; for the birds were like my dream,
And the leaves on the tree:

And the dear stainless buds of spring,
When upward they did move;
And many another gentle thing
Seemed fit for life and love.

And here and there someone would play,
Or make so fine a song
That all my sorrow fled away,
And there was nothing wrong.

But in the life the people led,
With sorrow day and night,
Vast wars, babes slaughtered, wicked bread—
O there was nothing right.

Then do you hate your being,
Curse the day you were born?
No, for another seeing
Makes me not all forlorn.

No matter what the body felt,
No matter what it saw,
My inmost spirit ever knelt
In a blind love and awe:

And dead or living knows full well
Sick or whole it knows,
The secret it may never tell
Of joy and of repose.

Ruth Pitter

THE REBELLIOUS VINE

One day, the vine
That clomb on God's own house
Cried, 'I will not *grow*.'
And, 'I will *not* grow,'
And 'I *will* not grow,'
And, '*I* will not grow.'
So God leaned out his head,
And said:
'You need not.' Then the vine
Fluttered its leaves, and cried to all the winds:

'Oh, have I not permission from the Lord?
And may I not begin to cease to grow?'
But that wise God had pondered on the vine
Before he made it
And, all the while it laboured *not* to grow,
It grew; it grew;
And all the time God knew.

Harold Monro

THREE BLESSINGS

(1)

The peace of joys,
The peace of lights,
The peace of consolations.

The peace of souls,
The peace of heaven,
The peace of virgins.

The peace of the fairy bowers,
The peace of peacefulness,
The peace of everlasting.

(2)

Peace between neighbours,
Peace between kindred,
Peace between lovers,
　In love of the King of life.

Peace between person and person,
Peace between wife and husband,
Peace between woman and children,
The peace of Christ above all peace.

Bless, O Christ, my face,
　Let my face bless everything;
Bless, O Christ, mine eye,
　Let mine eye bless all it sees.

(3)

The peace of God, the peace of men,
The peace of Columba kindly,
The peace of Mary mild, the loving,
    The peace of Christ, King of tenderness.

Be upon each window, upon each door,
Upon each hole that lets in light,
Upon the four corners of my house,
Upon the four corners of my bed,
    Upon the four corners of my bed;

Upon each thing my eye takes in,
Upon my body that is of earth
And upon my soul that came from on high,
    Upon my body that is of earth
    And upon my soul that came from on high.

Translated from the Gaelic by Alexander Carmichael

Part XVI

PRINCE OF PEACE

PRINCE OF PEACE

For unto us a Child is born, unto us a Son is given: and the government shall be upon his shoulder: and his name shall be called Wonderful, Counsellor, The mighty God, The everlasting Father, the Prince of Peace.

Isaiah IX 6

IN TERRA NOSTRA

By brake unleaved and hedgerow
Alight with barren thorn,
Along our English byways
The Son of God is born.

Where northern mountains muster
In steely grip their chain,
Or nursed by gentler hillocks
That hold a Suffolk lane:

On Cotswold ridge of splendour
By fretted music crowned,
Or where the streams meander
Through marshy Kentish ground;

In rain that clogs the earthways
Or snow on timid wings
A Manger stands erected
To house the King of Kings.

Alan C. Tarbat

FOR THE NATIVITY

Shepherds, I sing you, this winter's night
Our Hope new-planted, the womb'd, the buried Seed:
For a strange Star has fallen, to blossom from a tomb,
And infinite Godhead circumscribed, hangs helpless at the
   breast.

Now the cold airs are musical, and all the ways of the sky
Vivid with moving fires, above the hills where tread
The feet—how beautiful!—of them that publish peace.

The sacrifice, which is not made for them,
The angels comprehend, and bend to earth
Their worshipping way. Material kind Earth
Gives Him a Mother's breast, and needful food.

A Love, shepherds, most poor,
And yet most royal, kings,
Begins this winter's night;
But oh, cast forth, and with no proper place,
Out in the cold He lies!

John Heath-Stubbs

CHRISTMAS LANDSCAPE

Tonight the wind gnaws
with teeth of glass,
the jackdaw shivers
in caged branches of iron,
the stars have talons.

There is hunger in the mouth
of vole and badger,
silver agonies of breath
in the nostril of the fox,
ice on the rabbit's paw.

Tonight has no moon,
no food for the pilgrim;
the fruit tree is bare,
the rose bush a thorn
and the ground bitter with stones.

But the mole sleeps, and the hedgehog
lies curled in a womb of leaves,
the bean and the wheat-seed
hug their germs in the earth
and the stream moves under ice.

Tonight there is no moon,
but a new star opens
like a silver trumpet over the dead.
Tonight in a nest of ruins
the blessed babe is laid.

And the fir tree warms to a bloom of candles,
the child lights his lantern,
stares at his tinselled toy;
our hearts and hearths
smoulder with live ashes.

In the blood of our grief
the cold earth is suckled,
in our agony the womb
convulses its seed,
in the cry of anguish
the child's first breath is born.

Laurie Lee

THE GUEST

Tall, cool and gentle, you are here
To turn the water into wine.
Now, at the ebbing of the year,
Be you the sun we need to shine.

It is the birthday of your word;
And we are gathered. Will you come?
Let not your spirit be a sword,
O luminous delightful lord.

Harold Monro

PENTECOST

Love, we have spread the flowers here for your return.
The bread is baked, the water sweetly drawn,
the lamp is tended and the table laid.
　　Two candles burn
beside the empty glass and the silent wine.

The fire twists warm fingers in its smoky hair.
The door is open to the quiet crowds of night.
Stars thatch the sky above the continents'
　　divided lakes
with dark and crystal, all the foliage of light.

O, in this moment, endless as a warning dream,
the word we cannot speak may rouse us like a cry of pain.
Will you, too, with tongue of fire, be dumb?
　　When will your wine
speak in our veins again? Love, when will you come?

James Kirkup

THE GOOD SHEPHERD WITH THE KID

He saves the sheep, the goats he doth not save.
So rang Tertullian's sentence, on the side
Of that unpitying Phrygian sect which cried:
'Him can no fount of fresh forgiveness lave,

'Who sins, once wash'd by the baptismal wave.'—
So spake the fierce Tertullian. But she sigh'd,
The infant Church! of love she felt the tide
Stream on her from her Lord's yet recent grave.

And then she smiled; and in the Catacombs,
With eye suffused but heart inspired true,
On those walls subterranean, where she hid
Her head 'mid ignominy, death, and tombs,
She her good Shepherd's hasty image drew—
And on his shoulders, not a lamb, a kid.

Matthew Arnold

THE DIVINE IMAGE

To Mercy, Pity, Peace and Love
All pray in their distress:
And to these virtues of delight
Return their thankfulness.

For Mercy, Pity, Peace and Love
Is God, our Father dear,
And Mercy, Pity, Peace and Love
Is Man, His child and care.

For Mercy has a human heart,
Pity a human face,
And Love, the human form divine,
And Peace, the human dress.

Then every man, of every clime,
That prays in his distress,
Prays to the human form divine,
Love, Mercy, Pity, Peace.

And all must love the human form,
In heathen, Turk, or Jew;
Where Mercy, Love, and Pity dwell,
There God is dwelling too.

William Blake

Here in the self is all that man can know
Of Beauty, all the wonder, all the power,
All the unearthly colour, all the glow
Here in the self which withers like a flower;
Here in the self which fades as hours pass,
And droops and dies and rots and is forgotten
Sooner, by ages, then the mirroring glass
In which it sees its glory still unrotten.
Here in the flesh, within the flesh, behind,
Swift in the blood and throbbing on the bone,
Beauty herself, the universal mind,
Eternal April wandering alone;
The God, the holy God, the atoning Lord,
Here in the flesh, the never yet explored.

John Masefield

Here is thy footstool and there rest thy feet where live the
poorest, and lowliest, and best.
When I try to bow to thee, my obeisance cannot reach down
to the depth where thy feet rest among the poorest,
and lowliest, and lost.

Pride can never approach to where thou walkest in the
clothes of the humble among the poorest, and lowliest,
and lost.
My heart can never find its way to where thou keepest
company with the companionless among the poorest,
the lowliest, and the lost.

Leave this chanting and singing and telling of beads!
Whom does thou worship in this dark corner of a temple with
doors all shut?
Open thine eyes and see thy God is not before thee!
He is there where the tiller is tilling the hard ground and where
the path-maker is breaking stones. He is with them in
sun and in shower, and his garment is covered with
dust. Put off thy holy mantle even like him and come
down on the dusty soil!

Deliverance? Where is this deliverance to be found? Our master
    himself has joyfully taken upon him the bonds of
    creation; he is bound with us all forever.
Come out of thy meditations and leave aside thy flowers and
    incense; What harm is there if thy clothes become
    tattered and stained? Meet him and stand by him in
    toil and in the sweat of thy brow.

Rabindranath Tagore

'THROUGH THE DEAR MIGHT OF HIM
THAT WALKED THE WAVES'

For the sea, too, has its roads:
Beneath the swell, the restless whelm, her womb,
Flanked by those skeleton stone forests, where
Polyp and holothurian trail their tentacles.
The sea too has its alleys, highways, forums;
And thither throng
The sad, pale population of the drowned.
Riding the slow ground-currents like sleep-walkers:
Slim boys tricked out in shells and weed; old men
Out of long-foundered ships, whose coffers
Gape—a sardonic smile of gold and rubies;
Those who went down with bags of dates and raisins,
Or crates from Jaffa; the solitary airman
Who fell, a black bolt from a sky of fire,
Into the silent sea; the Punic sailor
Clutching his statues of the Cabiri,
Which once, upon his prow,
Gazed home to Carthage with dull wooden eyes,
And could not save in that last storm off Gades;
And here comes sidling by
A Portuguese lady with long bony hands,
Who sailed to join her bridegroom in Brazil,
In ragged satin (and a barnacle
Grows on her finger like a signet ring).
Here are the chiefs of Lyonesse, the bellringers

Of Ys, that famous town, and, grave
In their strange figured breastplates, senators
Of lost Atlantis,—
With all that former world which the first Flood
Had borne away, when under God's small stars,
In his great loneliness,
Noah weighed his anchor and set forth
On the dark sea. So, drifting past,
All names, known and unknown, she has sucked in:
The poor youth carried down the Dardanelles,
The poet, sunk without trace off Mexico.
And the drowned Lycidas.

This was the world that once Alcyone saw,
When in her sleep the phantom spread its wings,
And showed her dripping husband's dreary form.
Shelley was once a guest here, and the winds
And waves that carried his quenched ashes from the shore
Mingle them with it yet.
Poe in his dreams beheld the steep black wall
Of the gyrating maelström draw him down
And down and down into oblivion;
And Melville never could forget this nation,
But through his turgid water-world of thought
Still moved a white and awful shape,
The great sea-monster, the unconquered evil.

The ice-bergs, the blue cows of giantland,
Groaned as they clashed together through the night
And the cold mists, while the god Thor went out
To fish for the sea-serpent. But it lies
Coiled in the crater of a sunk volcano,
Watching with cruel and unwinking pupils
The little fishes, red and blue and yellow,
Go speeding past, with eager teeth to tear
The flesh of the young parricide, sewn in his sack,
And washed some three miles out from Ostia.
And there the mermaids' heartless song
Will madden and distract
The drowned man's slumbers in the deep-sea cave;
And there the Kraken waves its livid arms.

'Oh I would I were a halcyon-bird,
Beating with dark wings over the sea,
Whom the young ones carry when his years are done,
That bird of Spring. . . . 'Carry me to those feet
That tread unharvested Gennesaret's
Whitening wave-tops like the mountain dawn—
Above this monstrous world of squid and skate,
Sea-anemone, echinus and crinoid!
For I would see, outlined against the stars,
The Eternal Man measure with confidence
The treacherous foam-paths like a glossy pavement,
Who with His clear eyes looks down and sees
The sandy bottom and its life of slime—
All those dumb goggle-faces—
Assume the ordering of adoration.
And now His hand (which shall, at the end of time,
Capture Leviathan, and draw him forth
With bright gold scales glittering in the sun,
And land him gasping on the beach, to feed
Five thousand of the faithful)
Is stretched above the waves, to pluck
The failing Peter from their cold embrace.

John Heath-Stubbs

THE TRANSFIGURATION

So from the ground we felt that virtue branch
Through all our veins till we were whole, our wrists
As fresh and pure as water from a well,
Our hands made new to handle holy things,
The source of all our seeing rinsed and cleansed
Till earth and light and water entering there
Gave back to us the clear unfallen world.
We would have thrown our clothes away for lightness,
But that even they, though sour and travel stained,
Seemed like our flesh, made of immortal substance,
And the soiled flax and wool lay light upon us
Like friendly wonders, flower and flock entwined

As in a morning field. Was it a vision?
Or did we see that day the unseeable
One glory of the everlasting world
Perpetually at work, though never seen
Since Eden locked the gate that's everywhere
And nowhere? Was the change in us alone,
And the enormous earth still left forlorn,
An exile or a prisoner? Yet the world
We saw that day made this unreal, for all
Was in its place. The painted animals
Assembled there in gentle congregations,
Or sought apart their leafy oratorios,
Or walked in peace, the wild and tame together,
As if, also for them, the day had come.
The shepherds' hovels shone, for underneath
The soot we saw the stone clean at the heart
As on the starting-day. The refuse heaps
Were grained with that fine dust that made the world;
For he had said, 'To the pure all things are pure.'
And when we went into the town, he with us,
The lurkers under doorways, murderers,
With rags tied round their feet for silence, came
Out of themselves to us and were with us,
And those who hide within the labyrinth
Of their own loneliness and greatness came,
And those entangled in their own devices,
The silent and the garrulous liars, all
Stepped out of their dungeons and were free.
Reality or vision, this we have seen.
If it had lasted but another moment
It might have held for ever! But the world
Rolled back into its place, and we are here,
And all that radiant kingdom lies forlorn,
As if it had never stirred; no human voice
Is heard among its meadows, but it speaks
To itself alone, alone it flowers and shines
And blossoms for itself while time runs on.

But he will come again, it's said, though not
Unwanted and unsummoned; for all things,
Beasts of the field, and woods, and rocks, and seas,

And all mankind from end to end of the earth
Will call him with one voice. In our own time,
Some say, or at a time when time is ripe.
Then he will come, Christ the uncrucified,
Christ the discrucified, his death undone,
His agony unmade, his cross dismantled—
Glad to be so—and the tormented wood
Will cure its hurt and grow into a tree
In a green springing corner of your Eden,
And Judas damned takes his long journey backward
From darkness into light and be a child
Beside his mother's knee, and the betrayal
Be quite undone and never more be done.

Edwin Muir

THE OLIVE GARDEN

And still he climbed, and through the grey leaves thrust,
quite grey and lost in the grey olive lands,
and laid his burning forehead full of dust
deep in the dustiness of burning hands.

After all, this. And, this, then, was the end.
Now I'm to go, while I am going blind,
and, oh, why wilt Thou have me still contend
Thou art, whom I myself no longer find.

No more I find Thee. In myself no tone
of Thee; nor in the rest; nor in this stone.
I can find Thee no more. I am alone.

I am alone with all that human fate
I undertook through Thee to mitigate,
Thou who art not. Oh, shame too consummate . . .

An angel came, those afterwards relate.

Wherefore an angel? Oh, there came the night,
and turned the leaves of trees indifferently,

and the disciples stirred uneasily.
Wherefore an angel? Oh, there came the night.

The night that came requires no specifying;
just so a hundred nights go by,
while dogs are sleeping and while stones are lying—
just any melancholy night that, sighing,
lingers till morning mount the sky.

For angels never come to such men's prayers,
nor nights for them mix glory with their gloom.
Forsakenness is the self-loser's doom,
and such are absent from their father's cares
and disincluded from their mother's womb.

Rainer Maria Rilke.

THE VISION OF THE HOLY CHURCH

On all that the Lord laboured He lavished His love.
Love is the plant of peace, most precious of virtues;
All heaven could not hold it, so heavy in itself,
It fell in fulness forth on the field of earth
And of the folds of that field took flesh and blood;
No leaf thereafter on a linden-tree was ever lighter,
No needle-point so piercing or nimbler to handle,
No armour can withhold it or high wall hinder.
Therefore is Love leader of the Lord's folk in heaven,
And, to know its nature, it is nurtured in power,
And in the heart is it home and fountain-head.
Instinctively at heart a strength is stirring
Flowing to the Father that formed us all,
Looked on us with love, and let his Son die,
Meekly, for our misdoings, to amend us all.
Yet appointed He no punishment for the pain they put Him to,
But meekly with His mouth besought mercy for them,
And pity for the people that were putting Him to death.
See it an example, only seen in Him,
That He was mighty and yet meek, and had mercy to grant

298

To those that hung him on high and thrust him through the
    heart.
So I recommend you rich ones to have pity on the poor.
William Langland

THE KILLING

That was the day they killed the Son of God
On a squat hill-top by Jerusalem.
Zion was bare, her children from their maze
Sucked by the demon curiosity
Clean through the gates. The very halt and blind
Had somehow got themselves up to the hill.

After the ceremonial preparation,
The scourging, nailing, nailing against the wood,
Erection of the main-trees with their burden,
While from the hill rose an orchestral wailing,
They were there at last, high up in the soft spring day.

We watched the writhings, heard the moanings, saw
The three heads turning on their separate axles
Like broken wheels left spinning. Round *his* head
Was loosely bound a crown of plaited thorn
That hurt at random, stinging temple and brow
As the pain swung into its envious circle.
In front the wreath was gathered in a knot
That as he gazed looked like the last stump left
Of a death-wounded deer's great antlers. Some
Who came to stare grew silent as they looked,
Indignant or sorry. But the hardened old
And the hard-hearted young, although at odds
From the first morning, cursed him with one curse,
Having prayed for a Rabbi or an armed Messiah
And found the Son of God. What use to them
Was a God or a Son of God? Of what avail
For purposes such as theirs? Beside the cross-foot,
Alone, four women stood and did not move

All day. The sun revolved, the shadow wheeled,
The evening fell. His head lay on his breast,
But in his breast they watched his heart move on
By itself alone, accomplishing its journey.
Their taunts grew louder, sharpened by the knowledge
That he was walking in the park of death,
Far from their rage. Yet all grew stale at last,
Spite, curiosity, envy, hate itself.
They waited only for death and death was slow
And came so quietly they scarce could mark it.
They were angry then with death and death's deceit.

I was a stranger, could not read these people
Or this outlandish deity. Did a God
Indeed in dying cross my life that day
By chance, he on his road and I on mine?

Edwin Muir

THE HARROWING OF HELL

Painless at last, his being escaped from the terrible
body of pain. Upwards. Left it.
And lonely Dark was afraid
and flung at the pallor
bats in whose evening flitting there flutters still
fear of colliding
with that chilled anguish. Dim restless air
Depressed itself on the corpse, while gloomy aversion
rose in the powerful vigilant creatures of night.
His discharged spirit, perhaps, had thought of remaining
inactively, in the landscape. The immeasurable act of his
   suffering
would last him awhile. There was measure,
he felt, in the cool nocturnal presence of things
he now, like a lonely space, began to enclose.
But Earth, parched up in the thirst of his wounds, split open,
Earth split open, and all profundity thundered.
He, passed master in torments, heard all Hell

howling for confirmation
of his completed pain: that her continuing torture
might tremble at hint of an end in the end of his endless.
And, ghost as he was, he plunged with the downward weight
of all his weariness: hastily strode
through the startled backward stare of pasturing shadows,
hastily lifted his eyes to Adam
hastened down, disappeared, gleamed, vanished in plunging
of wilder depths. Suddenly (higher, higher), above the centre
of surging cries, stepped out on the top
of his tall unrailinged tower of endurance: breathless:
stood, surveyed his estate of Pain, was silent.

Rainer Maria Rilke

RESURRECTION

Sweet Peace, where dost thou dwell? I humbly crave
        Let me once know.
   I sought thee in a secret cave,
       And ask'd if Peace were there.
A hollow wind did seem to answer, 'No;
        Go seek elsewhere.'

I did; and going did a rainbow note:
        Surely, thought I,
   This is the lace of Peace's coat:
       I will search out the matter.
But while I look'd, the clouds immediately
        Did break and scatter.

Then went I to a garden, and did spy
        A gallant flower,
   The Crown Imperial. Sure, said I,
       Peace at the root must dwell.
But when I digg'd, I saw a worm devour
        What show'd so well.

At length I met a rev'rend good old man,
   Whom when for Peace
  I did demand, he thus began:
   'There was a Prince of old
At Salem dwelt, Who liv'd with good increase
   Of flock and fold.

'He sweetly liv'd; yet sweetness did not save
   His life from foes.
  But after death out of His grave
   There sprang twelve stalks of wheat;
Which many wond'ring at, got some of those
   To plant and set.

'It prosper'd strangely, and did soon disperse
   Through all the earth;
  For they that taste it do rehearse
   That virtue lies therein;
A secret virtue, bringing peace and mirth
   By flight of sin.

'Take of this grain, which in my garden grows,
   And grows for you;
  Make bread of it; and that repose
   And peace, which ev'ry where
With so much earnestness you do pursue,
   Is only there.'

George Herbert

CANTICLE OF THE SUN
DANCING ON EASTER MORNING

I am the great Sun. This hour begins
My dancing day—pirouetting in a whirl of white light
In my wide orchestral sky, a red ball bouncing
Across the eternal hills;
For now my Lord is restored: with the rising dew
He carries his own up to his glittering kingdom—
Benedicite, benedicite, benedicite omnia opera.

Look, I am one of the morning stars, shouting for joy—
And not the least honoured among those shining brothers,
O my planetary children—now that my dark daughter,
The prodigal Earth, is made an honest woman of;
Out of her gapped womb, her black and grimy tomb,
Breaks forth the Crowned, victory in his pierced hands—
Benedicite, benedicite, benedicite omnia opera.

You too, my lovers—little lark with trembling feathers,
Sing your small heart out in my streaming rays;
And you, grave narrow-browed eagle, straining your eyes
Against my wound—foretell
These fiery dales and flame-anemoned meadows
Shall be a haunt for shy contemplative spirits—
Benedicite, benedicite, benedicite omnia opera.

And now with joy I run my recurring race;
And though again I shall have to hide my face
With a hand of cloud out of the heart of schism,
Yet the time is sure when I once more shall be
A burning giant in his marriage-chamber,
A bright gold cherub, as I came from my Father's halls—
Benedicite, benedicite, benedicite omnia opera.

John Heath-Stubbs

MALLE AND WAT SEE A VISION

By now He had come nearly to the gate in the wall that
divided the Prioryland just here from the Bulmers'. He went
slowly, with His head bent, as though He marked the young
grass growing, for it was a very fair bright day, and for the
first time the grass smelt of spring. After Him, but some way
behind, came Malle and Wat. The brown ducks that had been
preening and scratching and shaking themselves with much
fuss and flutter on the edge of the pond went now in line,
following Him towards the gate, and a few of the Priory sheep,
which the shepherd had brought down from Owlands, moved
that way too, slowly, with little pauses and starts.

When the Man had gone through the gate, letting the weight swing it to after Him, He turned for a moment and looked at them all. They stood still, nor did any of those creatures move again until He went on, more quickly now, up the Nuns' Steps and into the wood.

Only then they came to the gate, and Malle and Wat stood looking over it and watching Him as He went. The ducks gathered about their feet, and the sheep too in a little crowd, and looked between the poles. The sun, not yet very high, struck right in among the bare trees, finding out the bright watery green of the trunks, and unlocking all the distances. The wind, moving strongly through the wood, filled it with sliding shadows, as if the air bore light upon its back as a running river bears ripples. So He went up and out of sight, under the great branches that bowed and swung, while the little twigs seemed to clap themselves together for joy.

A cloud covered the sun. He had gone, and Malle and Wat came back to the bare hillside among the boulders, where now the wind brought only chill. But for Malle it was golden harvest weather; the ears of corn were full, wrought four-square, firm as a rope, exact as goldsmiths' work; like rope ends they struck her thighs as she moved through them, loaded with goodness.

She plumped down on the ground, and caught Wat by his knees so that he tumbled against her. Then they sat together, rocking to and fro, and Malle kept on babbling, 'We shall brast, Wat, we shall brast,' while Wat made shocking faces and groaned in his throat; it hurt them so, the joy that was far too big for them, and the dread. For God, that was too great to be holden even of everywhere and forever, had bound Himself into the narrow room of here and now. He that was in all things had, for pity, prisoned Himself in flesh and in simple bread. He that thought winds, waters and stars, had made of Himself a dying man.

But at last, as if it were a great head of water that had poured itself with noise, and splashing, and white foam leaping into a pool, and now, rising higher, covered its own inflow, and so ran silent, though no less strong—now they were lifted up and borne lightly as a fisherman's floats, and as stilly.

They crouched on the hillside, looking towards God, feeling God under their spread palms on the grass, and through the soles of their feet. Beyond, beyond, beyond, and beyond again, yet always that which went still beyond—God. And here, with only a low wooden gate between, that thing which man could never of himself have thought, and would never come to the depth of for all his thinking, here that thing impossible was true as daylight, here was God in man, here. All in a point.

ROBERT ASKE DIES IN CHAINS AT YORK

Thunder came after dark and with it rain, a rushing sluice of unseen waters that mashed down great swathes of the tall, heady-heavy wheat. Rain beating on his head and neck brought Aske back for a little while out of nightmare into conscious horror. He saw in the scribble of lightning which split black night the sheer drop of the wall beside him; the green far away below.

And as his eye told him of the sickening depth below his body, and his mind forknew the lagging endlessness of torment before him, so, as if the lightning had brought an inner illumination also, he knew the greater gulf of despair above which his spirit hung, helpless and aghast.

God did not now, nor would in any furthest future, prevail. Once He had come, and died. If He came again, again He would die, and again, and so for ever, by His own will rendered powerless against the free and evil wills of men.

Then Aske met the full assault of darkness without reprieve of hoped for light, for God ultimately vanquished was no God at all. But yet, though God was not God, as the head of the dumb worm turns, so his spirit turned, blindly, gropingly, hopelessly loyal, towards that good, that holy, that merciful, which though not God, though vanquished, was still the last dear love of a vanquished and tortured man.

*   *   *

Then Malle said:
'The darkness is done. The sun's risen, just one morning like any other sunshine morning, with folks about their business and wives baking bread, and the mill-wheel turning. It's all light in the churchyard, young new light, the colour of green apples when they're golding over.'

Wat crept a little nearer, but he was shaking.

'God 'a mercy!' Malle cried. 'God 'a mercy! Here He comes between the graves, out of the grave.

'When He was born a man,' she said, 'He put on the leaden shroud that's man's dying body. And on the Cross it bore Him down, sore heavy, dragging against the great nails, muffling God, blinding Him to the blindness of a man. But there, darkened within that shroud of mortal lead, beyond the furthest edge of hope, God had courage to trust yet in hopeless, helpless things, in gentle mercy, holiness, love crucified.

'And that courage, Wat, it was too rare and keen and quick a thing for sullen lead to prison, but instead it broke through, thinning lead, fining it to purest shining glass, to be a lamp for God to burn in.

'So men may have courage,' she said, and caught Wat by the skirt of his coat as she stood up. 'Then they will see how bright God shines. Come,' she said, dragging Wat towards the door, 'and tell him that's been taken far from here to die.'

* * *

But Robert Aske had gone too far, nor did he need now that Malle should tell him.

For now (yet with no greater fissure between then and now than as a man's eyes are aware, where no star was, of the first star of night), now he was aware of One—vanquished God, Saviour who could as little save others as Himself.

But now, beside Him and beyond was nothing, and He was silence and light.

H. F. M. Prescott

EMMAUS

Not while they walked, though he seemed strangely sure
when first he fell into their company,
and passed before them through the lowly door
with more than manliest solemnity;
not while they laid the table, rather flurried,
and half-ashamed of what he'd come to share,
and he stood tolerantly, with his unhurried
spectatorship reposing on the pair;

not even when, eager to break the ice,
they'd settled down, convivially waiting,
and he had grasped the bread, with hesitating,
beautiful hands, to do, within a trice,
what should convulse them into vast relation,
like terror leaping through a crowded street—
not till they'd seen, before that large donation,
the narrow limits of their meal retreat,
they knew, and, rapt into intenser living,
arose with bended head and trembling knee.
Then, when they saw he'd not yet finished giving,
forthreached for the two mouthfuls, quiveringly.

Rainer Maria Rilke

NO BEAUTY WE COULD DESIRE

Yes, you are always everywhere. But I,
Hunting in such immeasurable forests,
Could never bring the noble Hart to bay.

The scent was too perplexing for my hounds;
Nowhere sometimes, then again everywhere.
Other scents, too, seemed to them almost the same.

Therefore I turn my back on the unapproachable
Stars and horizons and all musical sounds,
Poetry itself, and all the winding stair of thought.

Leaving the forests where you are pursued in vain
—Often a mere white gleam—I turn instead
To the appointed place where you pursue.

Not in Nature, not even in Man, but in one
Particular Man, with a date, so tall, weighing
So much, talking Aramaic, having learned a trade;

Not in all food, not in all bread and wine
(Not, I mean, as my littleness requires)
But this wine, this bread . . . no beauty we could desire.

C. S. Lewis

THE UNKNOWN GOD

One of the crowd went up,
And knelt before the Paten and the Cup,
Received the Lord, returned in peace, and prayed
Close to my side. Then in my heart I said:

'O Christ, in this man's life—
This stranger who is Thine—in all his strife,
All his felicity, his good and ill,
In the assaulted stronghold of his will,

'I do confess Thee here,
Alive within this life; I know Thee near
Within this lonely conscience, closed away
Within this brother's solitary day.

'Christ in his unknown heart,
His intellect unknown—this love, this art,
This battle and this peace, this destiny
That I shall never know, look upon me!

'Christ in his numbered breath,
Christ in his beating heart and in his death,
Christ in his mystery! From that secret place
And from that separate dwelling, give me grace!'

Alice Meynell

He comes to us as One unknown, without a name, as of old,
by the lakeside, He came to those men who knew Him not. He
speaks to us the same word: 'Follow thou me!' and sets us the
tasks which He has to fulfil for our time. He commands. And
to those who obey Him, whether they be wise or simple, He
will reveal Himself in the toils, the conflicts, the sufferings
which they will pass through in His fellowship, and, as an
ineffable mystery, they shall learn in their own experience Who
He is.

Albert Schweitzer   from The Quest of the Historical Jesus

THE QUESTION

Will you, sometime, who have sought so long and seek
Still in the slowly darkening hunting ground,
Catch sight some ordinary month or week
Of that strange quarry you scarcely thought you sought—
Yourself, the gatherer gathered, the finder found,
The buyer, who would buy all, in bounty bought—
And perch in pride on the princely hand, at home,
And there, the long hunt over, rest and roam?

Edwin Muir

INDEX OF AUTHORS

312

INDEX OF FIRST LINES